A Religion of Story

A Powerful Way to Cultivate
Character and Preserve Freedom
in Our Children and Culture

by
Amanda Johnson & Aaron Johnson

Saved By Story

A Religion of Story

A Powerful Way to Cultivate Character and Preserve
Freedom in Our Children and Culture

Published by
Saved By Story Publishing, LLC
Prescott, AZ

www.SavedByStory.house

Illustration by Eshaal Kashif
Cover Design by Lionheart Creations
Interior Design by Dawn Teagarden

ISBN: Paperback 978-0-9887809-3-4

Hard Cover 978-0-9887809-5-8

Printed in the United States of America

www.SavedByStory.house

To Ryan / Dad
You sparked this at that dinner table long ago.
It's definitely all your fault.
And, thank you!

Acknowledgments

To Ryan/Dad, we know it is not easy to hang out with us story junkies. Thank you for all of your support and insight along the way. We won't tell anyone that we've nearly pulled you all the way onto the dark side and made you a story junkie, too. ☺

To the on-and-off-screen Mentors and Allies who have played such a huge part of our own heroes' journeys. Where would we be without you and the superpowers you bring to our lives? Alyssa, thank you for your part in the epic book cover. Theddee, thank you for the whooping and hollering you did as you read through the initial drafts.

To the on-and-off-screen Villains who have played such key roles in developing our character and teaching us to preserve our freedom *and* understand Redemption. We have done our best to pay our deepest respects to you on these pages.

To the Co-Author that oh-so-perfectly inserts the movies, tv shows, and real-life characters needed to compel us further into our Destiny, and keeps The Unknown so damn interesting and fun.

To the on-and-off-screen Leaders and Fellowships who are always developing our capacity for whatever is next.

And of course, to the Authors of our favorite books, movies, and tv shows for changing our lives by dedicating *their* lives to creating something more than "just stories" — whether they knew what they were doing or not.

With All Our Love and Gratitude,

Amanda & Aaron Johnson

Contents

Sam: "I wonder if we'll ever be put into songs or tales. I wonder if people will ever say, 'Let's hear about Frodo and the Ring.' And they'll say 'Yes, that's one of my favorite stories. Frodo was really courageous, wasn't he, Dad?' 'Yes, my boy, the most famousest of hobbits. And that's saying a lot.'"

Frodo: "You've left out one of the chief characters — Samwise the Brave. I want to hear more about Sam. Frodo wouldn't have got far without Sam."

Sam: "Now, Mr. Frodo, you shouldn't make fun; I was being serious."

Frodo: "So was I."

Sam: "Samwise the Brave..."

~ J.R.R. Tolkien, The Two Towers ~

The Language of Story

By Kate Herr, PsyD

"You should write. You're so good at it!" she said, for what felt like the millionth time.

It was another texting conversation between me and one of my dearest, and by far, oldest friends. She is known to many as Amanda Johnson, CEO of True to Intention and Messenger Guide. But to me, she is Mandy, aka, my Mr. Frodo. Though we were only texting, I'm sure she heard the cynical tone coming from my soul and could feel the roll of my eyes. See, I'm just Samwise and my Mr. Frodo has been insisting that I write a book because she is convinced that I have some amazing story to tell that will help others in the great Novel we all play a part in, not unlike Samwise of *The Lord of the Rings*. You know, at the end, when Frodo gives Sam the book to write the last few chapters. For years, maybe decades, and most definitely a few lifetimes, I have been sidestepping her encouragement (more like persistent and sometimes annoying nudges) to write. Why? I'm not as convinced as she is that the world would benefit from what I have to say, because I'm more of a listener. I'm a Sam, not a Frodo. But, here we are. And instead of asking me to finish the book, like Frodo asked Sam, Mandy has asked me to write a foreword. How could Sam ever say "no" to his Mr. Frodo.

Mandy and I met during those magical, crazy, and tumultuous years of adolescence. She was a year ahead of me in school and the smart, popular, and cool girl who everyone seemed to adore and envy. I, on the other hand, was the girl who was really into ceramics, cutting class to play with clay and leaving remnants of dust on the school desks, which often looked like dandruff. I got okay grades but had to work really hard for them. I didn't consider myself anything special, let alone smart. In fact, I had struggled with reading since I was a child. My writing skills weren't great. And math was my mortal enemy (and still is). For obvious reasons, Mandy and I didn't really run in the same social circles. We knew of each other, growing up in a small mountain community, but didn't really interact much until need drove us into friendship.

I'm not sh*tting you, Mandy and I became friends over her need for toilet paper while camping in a dusty field in Mexicali on a high school mission's trip. We walked the quarter of the mile back to camp and the latrines; and during that long walk, a lifelong and life-changing friendship emerged out of a rather mundane need. But, that is just where it started. Neither one of us could have imagined the journey we were about to embark upon, during which she would become my Mr. Frodo, and I, her Samwise — the journey from adolescence into adulthood.

Over the next decade, Mandy and I walked together as our worlds, our identities, and our faith were turned upside-down, inside-out, and left in ruin. (Don't worry, we've made it back from Mt. Doom, though I'm not sure we have landed back in the Shire just yet. And just to clarify, even the Shire needed saving once the brave hobbits returned home, at least according to the book.) It all started for me when she told me I was smart. It might sound funny, but this reflection rocked my world because it was so far from the story that had been reflected to me and the one I had begun to rehearse. Here was one of the smartest people I knew, telling me (a mediocre student who worked her ass off for Bs and Cs) that I was as smart, if not smarter than her in some ways. Mandy was so convinced of my smartness that she encouraged me to follow her into an honors program at a private university. I had always figured I'd go to some sort of college, but a private university and an honors program?!?! I didn't have the grades. I didn't have the academic acumen. But, she was so sure of my potential and smartness that she put her name and reputation on the line and backed me all the way, going so far as to petition the director of the honors program to let me in. And then poof, like magic, this mediocre student was enrolled in an honors program that engaged great books using the Socratic method. Fast-forward another decade, and that mediocre student who cut class to play with clay is now a Licensed Clinical Psychologist. Having earned a doctorate in psychology, I now spend my working hours helping people rewrite some of the most difficult and traumatic parts of their story. I can tell you, most emphatically, that humans are a species meant for storytelling and storymaking; and the mindfulness with which we encounter and write those stories can set the tone for generations to come.

So, how did these two unlikely allies get sucked into seeing the world, and our lives through the lens of story? (Images of Narnia's *Voyage of the Dawn Treader* coming to mind. You know, that scene when the kids get sucked into the picture of a ship sailing the seas.) Well, you will hear all about Mandy's journey into Story in the pages to come, but mine started with the superhero stories I engaged as a young child. Oftentimes, when I'd go visit my grandmother, my uncle Bobby would spend hours inventing and telling me superhero stories in which I would be the hero, "Princess Fate." As I got older, I was invited into co-creating the stories with him. He would set the scene with the daring adventure, introduce the challenge and the villain, and then it was my turn. As "Princess Fate," I had to decide how I was going to overcome the obstacles and defeat the bad guy. His stories were so engaging and inspiring that when it was time for me to go to bed, I would continue the adventures, daydreaming various scenarios until I drifted off to sleep. I'm now forty years old, a full-fledged adult, and I still fall asleep at night daydreaming of different adventures. Over the years, Princess Fate evolved into a Starfleet officer, a dragon rider, and as of late, the winner of a survivalist show called *Alone*. Some adults might find this admission embarrassing, but I don't for this simple reason: it keeps my imagination and creativity flexible, and that is crucial in maintaining psychological health and well-being.

Did you know that children are generally much more psychologically resilient than adults? Do you want to know why?

It's because they play and, in their play, can experiment, engage in creative and out-of-the-box thinking, and in doing so come to a resolution that would escape many adults who have lost that sense of "magical" thinking.

As Mandy and I made our way through the gauntlet of transitioning from adolescence into adulthood, we bonded over stories. The stories we read, the stories we watched unfold on screen, the stories that we'd been taught growing up, and the stories we were beginning to write for ourselves all blended together as we found ourselves leaving the Shire and heading into a journey that was way beyond our kin. Stories guided us, inspired us, and gave us a language and structure to talk about thoughts and feelings that were otherwise out of reach, despite our tremendous education. The language of Story allowed us to play more freely in our internal and external worlds as we evolved from being just characters in a story, to narrators, and now to co-authors. Story allowed us to keep our childhood imaginations in the adult game of life.

A few years into our exodus from the Shire, and right in the middle of being lost on our way to Mordor, Mr. Frodo (aka Mandy) had a kid! And that's when the sh*t got really REAL! We were still young adults, barely old enough to purchase liquor. Our external world had been shaken by 9-11, and our internal worlds felt much like Alice's after she fell through the looking glass. When up became down, and down was up — that's when Aaron joined the Fellowship. We were now responsible for this kiddo. Yes, I say "we" because I accepted the responsibility of keeping an eye on Mr. Frodo's offspring, 'cause that's what Samwise does. Of course, I wasn't Aaron's parent, but I had an important role to play, nonetheless. I was an aunt, of sorts. I set out to be that aunt who would help him get ready for the crazy world of adventures yet to come. I would challenge him, dare him to go just beyond his comfort zone, even cheat at games to help prepare him to take on the world. Basically, I would be a Merry to this young Pippin. I'd be there to get him into some (age appropriate) trouble, and I'd be there to help him figure out how to overcome it.

When I observed Mandy and Ryan beginning to use the language of Story to help Aaron develop critical thinking skills, empathy, the capacity of foreshadowing, and character-building, it was a no-brainer… of course! My studies of psychology, childhood development, philosophy, and religion all pointed to a universal theme of Story. Just think about it, before the invention of TV or even books, all one had to do after dark was sit around a fire and listen to the elders pass down the stories of those who came before them! This was how we, as a human species, first began to learn and experience a continuity of tradition, belonging, identity, purpose, and meaning. The use of Story has always been our human way of teaching, learning, and making sense of the world and our role in that world. So, why did it seem so novel? Because, TV started to tell the stories and for the most part, parents (aka the elders) were absent. They were too exhausted to engage and just wanted to relax, in another room altogether, or even worse, the parents had already lost their creativity and flexibility and were stuck thinking about a story from only one vantage point.

It's been eighteen years since young Mr. Pippin (Aaron) joined the Fellowship (gulp... the years have flown by!). While Mandy and I have many more adventures yet to come, soon the main adventures of this world will pass to Aaron (and his generation); such is the nature of Story, one generation declines and another emerges to march forward. But let's be honest, Aaron's generation will have a lot of leftover sh*t to sift through when it's time for them to take the lead roles.

How do we prepare them for this?

There are so many ways to answer this question. I would submit that one of the best ways we can prepare the next generation is by teaching them the art of Storytelling and Storymaking. We show them how to learn from the Stories of the past, both fiction and nonfiction. Not by indoctrinating them into a certain viewpoint from which to judge the Story and its characters. But, rather by teaching them to approach it with benign curiosity. Teaching them how to ask questions, and most especially the questions that are awkward and uncomfortable and invite vulnerability. We also must show them how to find hope and notice the invitations for redemption that exist in every story, despite the hardships encountered and the paths that lead into the wilderness of despair. How do we teach them these things? Story, of course! We teach by actively, mindfully, and humbly modeling the process of Story.

This is the invitation you will receive as you encounter the stories offered by Mandy and Aaron in this book. These two have vulnerably modeled the way they've encountered and relied upon Story as a means of passing along wisdom, hope, character, and fortitude within the parent/child relationship.

You might still be asking the question: How could understanding the skills of Storytelling and Storymaking make a difference in the development of a child?

I invite you to observe Aaron's development of applying critical thinking, foreshadowing, empathy, and character development as this book progresses. Notice the openness of dialogue between him and Mandy over the years and understand that you're just getting a small peek at the honest and pivotal conversations they've shared as parent and child. Can you imagine having open, non-defensive conversations with your parent or child? Remember as you read, at the time this book is being written Aaron is eighteen years old! How were you engaging, thinking, and feeling about the challenges of life at that age? How vulnerable were you willing to be about your internal thoughts and reflections? Most adolescents and young adults that I work with would be terrified at the prospect of co-authoring a book with their mother about their childhood. Talk about being put on "front street"!

I have witnessed, firsthand, how the language of Story has been instrumental in helping Aaron develop into a kind, resilient, smartass (in the right way), and funny man who is honest, vulnerable, and willing to step into brave unknowns with humility and strength. He is already engaging life on his own, empowered terms. Learning from the mistakes he has witnessed in stories, both fictional and in the lives of those who have gone before him. All while breaking through intergenerational curses and redefining what it means for him to be a successful entrepreneur, businessman, and even a leader. Don't get me wrong, Aaron still has A LOT of learning and growing and messing up to do. He is, after all, human. The point is, with the language of Story and the support of his comrades, Aaron has a robust and flexible way of understanding and engaging with the ups and downs, inevitable detours, and even successes on his life adventure.

*Isn't that what we all hope our kids will have
as they embark into adulthood?*

"Fiction isn't false — it's not a lie.

It's not literal, but it's not a lie.

And great fiction is true, but it never happened.

So how can it be true?

And the answer to that is something like: 'There are patterns in things. Deep patterns. Deep recurring patterns... The fact that we're human, that humanity itself is a recurring pattern; it has characteristic shape. And great fiction describes the shape of that pattern...'

The greater fiction becomes, the more it is religious in nature... and a story that can change your life has a power that is best described as religious..."

~ Dr. Jordan B. Peterson ~

Saved By Story

"**M**om, why don't we have a bible?" he asked as we sat down for dinner. Aaron's four-year-old voice always oozed curiosity, but not usually with this tone of concern.

Oh boy! He's been hanging out with the extended family again! I could feel the frustration simmering beneath my skin.

"We do have a bible. It's *Avatar: The Last Airbender,*" his dad interjected and shot me a quick wink and a smile across the table.

"Oh… well… okay…" The answer seemed to satisfy Aaron enough that he grabbed his fork and got lost in the food in front of him.

Avatar is our bible! OMG, that was genius! I thought as I smiled back at my husband and began eating. *It's true. That show has all of the most important life lessons wrapped up in a super fun adventure.*

My husband's quick thinking cracked open an idea that day — one that was confirmed and expanded as we neared the end of the cartoon series many years later.

We all sat in the oversized living room with the big screen tv, watching as the main character trained with his mentor. As he was preparing himself for the final battle, he had a vision that his friend was in trouble. Immediately, he stopped his training.

I leapt for the remote control, paused the show, and asked Aaron what he thought would happen if the hero stopped his training. After his frustrated "I don't know," I offered a clue from the *Star Wars* epic we had just finished watching the night before; and after a short line of inquiries, he predicted on his own that this hero was going to fail and/or get hurt in the process.

Looking back, I realize that the question itself was a huge risk. I hadn't seen this episode before. I didn't know for sure that the main character was going to walk into a trap and be almost-mortally wounded. But it all happened as I'd predicted.

Maybe I *did* know that it was going to happen. But how would I have known that?

Well, I didn't learn about story and archetypes until a decade after this moment in the oversized living room, but I didn't have to know what they were in order to experience their power.

Soon, I would discover that I already had a religion of Story and that it was time for me to refine it with the help of my son.

My Story

I, myself, was raised on the story of the ultimate hero— Jesus Christ.

I don't remember any religious conversations happening in my home in my early childhood, but that all changed when we moved to a small mountain community and I began attending a private Christian school.

I'm not sure what the impetus was for this decision. Maybe my mom decided I needed some moral guidance after our conversation about the birds and the bees, when she realized just how much time I had been spending with my much-older cousins at Gramma's house. Perhaps it was because she and my dad had just suffered a family rupture that led them to search for answers for how to set life right again. Maybe they didn't know how to help their sad little girl, who was clearly suffering from a broken heart after being moved (might as well have been a million) miles from the grandma who had been more like her best buddy for the first five years of her life. Whatever the reason was, I suddenly found myself interacting with religious stories for the first time in my life.

Unfortunately, in this particular community, the greatest love story ever told — the Creator of the Universe sending His only Son to save the world from sin — was a little heavy on the sin and the fear of hell for such a small child. Even more unfortunately, this story seemed to answer the questions that were plaguing my little mind and heart: Why do they get upset when I ask questions? Why is it so hard to make friends? What's wrong with me that their parents don't want me around? Why is it, no matter how hard I try, I don't feel okay? The answer from this religious community's doctrine was, "There's something essentially wrong with you. You're a sinner. You must be saved by grace... or else..."

I asked Jesus into my heart when I was seven years old during chapel after sitting wide-eyed and riveted by the stories of what happens to people who don't. Tears streamed down my face as I prayed and felt the terror being replaced by gratitude.

I spent the remainder of my elementary and secondary education in that small religious community. Sadly, accepting Jesus into my heart did *not* fix the problem of other kids not liking me; but I loved my teachers, performed well in school, and "saved" my beloved grandma when I was finally able to see her again. I felt grateful to have a relationship with my Creator, participate in sharing The Good News of the Gospel, and witness the miracles of healing, guidance, and provision that happened regularly.

Of course, I also struggled to make sense of the dramas in the churches we attended: pastors apologizing to the congregation for adultery, gossipy prayer chains, Bible-thumping leaders, etc. I lost track of the number of times I sat in the back of a car speeding out of a church parking lot, my mom muttering something to the effect of: "You can take your legalistic attitude and..."

Attuned to the reality of hypocrisy, or at least failure to live up to The Standard, I did my best to be a good Christian girl. Of course, I had my own run-in with the religious community my last year of high school. Falsely accused of misbehaving, I suffered quite the blow to my sense of belonging and was ready to leave what had been my home for twelve years to attend the Christian university of my choice.

It might as well have been the first question out of my professor's mouth because I don't remember anything that led up to it: "But how do you know that God really exists?" If not for the very real experience of public miracles and private moments with my Creator, I might have lost my faith that day because it wasn't really *my truth;* it was the set of beliefs I'd inherited. The next few years of the classic books program at the Christian university challenged me on every level. While most students at the school studied the Bible, we read through the most influential classic books in the western world (and some from the east). With every turn of the page and inquiry offered, I questioned every belief that had been so widely accepted back home. And as I pursued my teaching credential and learned about the power of the self-image and how it can be transformed, I made some decisions about how I would choose to walk through this world and interact with every person I met.

By the time Aaron surprised me with his arrival, I had come to several conclusions; but the ones that matter most to this conversation are these: 1) There are more similarities than differences in the world religions and their stories, and I prefer to live focused on embodying (rather than debating) the universal truths that bind all stories and humans together. 2) These truths permeate history and yet are shared through individual filters of experience; thus the importance of understanding the personal stories of the authors, artists, and other creators who are providing us with the means to understand our history. 3) An individual's body, mind, spirit, and journey are sacred; and my role in everyone's life is to focus on the divinity within them and witness their journey, not shape or carve it out for them.

Since these conclusions contradict (or at least challenge) many of the beliefs and practices with which I was raised, raising a child according to these principles while surrounded by extended family still operating under the old ones posed a few serious obstacles for me. Plus, our relationship was tenuous, as I'd been a bit of a nightmare for all of them in the first few years of university. While my whole world(view) seemed to be falling apart at the seams, I skipped the fear, went straight to anger, and began challenging, provoking, and burning bridges with people I loved and didn't know how to relate to anymore.

That's why, in addition to the normal lists moms provide when leaving their children with family — nap schedules, sugar restrictions, and behavior modification approaches — I made two more very firm requests with these brief explanations:

1. Never ever call him a bad boy. He's always good and worthy of love and respect, but sometimes his choices are not. When you correct him, address the choice, not his worth, please. (This was my attempt to not perpetuate the "there's something essentially wrong with you" belief.)

2. Refrain from indoctrination. Little minds believe most of what the adult people in their lives say, and we want him to make up his own mind about what he believes about God when he is old enough to think for himself on the matter. If he asks you a question about God, please start it with, "Well, *I* believe that…"

I was determined to protect his little mind and heart and preserve his choice in what I consider to be the most important and life-shaping question anyone could ever ask: Who is God?

Of course, as you have probably guessed because of the story you have already read, despite my attempts, he was still being introduced to religion through their practices; and I was feeling pretty frustrated that he was getting only one side of the story. That is, until my husband made the comment about this tv series being our Bible. Suddenly, I had a clear path to cultivating character and preserving his freedom: working through many stories with him the way I had learned to work through them in the honors program.

Our Story

As I write these words, Aaron is seventeen years old and our journey through Story continues. We spend most of our time together watching movies, television series, and videos and discussing writers' intentions, human development, relationships, and why such messages might be emerging at particular times in our personal and collective history. However, it wasn't until last year that I began to hear him formulating and articulating some of his own thoughts about the Laws of Nature and God.

I'm gonna let you witness his conclusions as they unfolded, but I'll tell you right now that there was a moment when we were watching a tv show together when he said something that told me he had arrived at some answers inside himself, and that his answers were not only a lot healthier for him at seventeen than mine were for me when I was that age, but they were also *really his.*

A tear slipped down my cheek as I recognized the feeling I was experiencing. It wasn't just momma pride. It was the same feeling that I had when he was three years old and corrected his angry gramma when she was scolding him: "I'm *not* bad. I just made a bad choice and I'm sorry." It was one of those moments in which I witnessed a generational matrix heal.

While this young man exudes all of the best qualities of those who have come before him, this process of working through stories together has allowed him to *free himself* from the unhealthy generational patterns, and *choose* the role he wants to play in his personal story and the bigger collective story.

After that conversation and those that followed in the next few months, as he connected the stories we had experienced with the information in some of his classes and on the news and articulated his thoughts out loud, I realized that our story needs to be told. In fact, this idea of raising a child on the religion of story might help other parents raising a child in a world that, as I write these words, is facing some of the toughest challenges in our history — a global pandemic, social unrest complete with peaceful protests *and* violent riots, and an election in which our country's future and our personal freedoms clearly hang in the balance.

Saving Ourselves Through Story

Preserving Valuable Foundations and Freedom

Most people know that stories, oral and written, have been the primary means of keeping cultures intact and evolving them across generations. These stories share their culture's understanding of the origin of humanity, the great floods and famines they've survived, the wars they have won and lost, the triumphs and falls of great leaders, the prophecies and predictions of the spiritual elders, and the wisdom they've gained from all of it. Through these stories, we understand the culture's values, beliefs, and traditions and how they are communicated, preserved, and often evolved or expanded upon from one generation to the next.

This means that, for millennia, stories have been the *primary way* we learn the most important lessons about our origin, the world around us, and who we are in relationship to all of it. Thus, we are naturally wired to learn from the stories we engage in any medium; and I believe we do learn from all of them, whether we are conscious of it or not. Depending on the story, and especially the author's intentions, this isn't necessarily *good* for us. Someone trying to steer a culture could easily write stories designed to teach lessons that would lead to the fulfillment of their selfish agenda rather than the expansion of human potential. This might be one of the most important reasons to bring a heightened level of awareness and inquiry to the stories you and your child engage. It's worth the eyerolls and frustrated sighs you'll experience when you start asking questions like, "What do you think the writer of this story is trying to say?"

Uncovering Strengths and Desires

As you'll see throughout the book, I spent a lot of our time asking questions and listening. Instead of telling Aaron what I thought about the plot and message, the characters and their choices, and the outcomes, I asked him for *his* perspective. I really wanted to know what he was thinking about all of it, especially since he didn't have the decades of accumulated filters between him and what was coming toward him. One of my favorite questions to ask was, "Who is your favorite character and why?" His answers were *never* what I expected or would have chosen myself, yet they gave me a little window into his developing perspective of what a hero looks and sounds like. I could hear his aspirations and his admiration of certain qualities of character over others, and it gave me incredible insight into what his natural inclinations and strengths were. This gave me so much momma power. When an opportunity presented itself, I would point out how that same quality was in him and smile when my little big man stood a little taller and prouder. Looking back, I can see how these qualities that he identified when he was a youngster are still at the top of his list and, no surprise, exactly what he will need to be the leader I've always known he is here to be.

Activating Potential

The way life and my education unfolded, I had a pretty decent understanding of the importance of cultivating and preserving a little person's sense of self with reasonably high expectations and choice. I also knew that because they are so little, and don't have a lot of life experience to prove otherwise, they have immense power to create through their imagination. Of course, engaging stories intentionally gives us lots of opportunities to expand our child's imagination and show them how to use it to create the life they want to live.

For example, Aaron hardly ever got sick as a child, and I'd like to think it was because I was always elevating his body's ability to "kill the bugs." However, about once a year, he would present a wicked high fever and tell me, "Mom, I don't feel very good. I'm going to start watching *Harry Potter*." When I'd ask why, he'd say, "I don't know. I always feel better when I'm done watching it." I'd ask if he thought it was the magic and he'd smile, nod, and turn on the tv. And, like clockwork, he would finish the series and suddenly his fever would be gone. Call it a Placebo Effect if you like, but it was predictable. To this day, it's his go-to when some sort of bug tries to take him down.

Healing Old St*ries and Shifting Generational Patterns

It's one thing to give your child the opportunity to engage stories and learn lessons that will help them steer clear of negative familial patterns, but it's another to engage the stories in a way that will help you to change the patterns in your life as well. As you read through this book, you'll find me in plenty of moments where I was face-to-face with the wounds and beliefs that had limited my life, sorting through the shrapnel with my son right there with me. Sometimes, I did this privately because the nature of the trauma and his age were not a match; but as he's gotten older and we've tackled some of the tougher conversations, I've been able to give him a window into his generational defaults and the opportunity to make a new choice.

Cultivating Character and Wisdom

I know that many family members and friends were rather concerned with my grand experiment with Aaron — my refusal to raise him with a particular dogma and instead expose him to universal truths through story — and now I have to stifle my laughter when I watch their faces as he shares his extremely moral opinions. The mandate that we should "train up a child in the way he should go, and when he is old, he will not depart from it" (Proverbs 22:6) is absolutely worthy of our effort; but I believe it's been misconstrued over time. In my small religious community, it meant "tell the child what is moral and immoral" rather than "raise your child to know the way to navigate the path wisely." Doesn't that make you feel a little scared? None of us want our child to learn through the school of hard knocks like we did, but experience is how we learn. My dad used to say, "Experience is that thing you need right before you get it." So, what if we could give our children the experience through story?

What if they could walk a million miles in other people's shoes? What if they could witness the big errors and the tiny ones and be guided to explore *why* someone might make a decision like that? What if they could see the consequences of all of them... repeatedly?

Then, they could do their own morality math: "These choices consistently lead to these outcomes, and I prefer not to experience that." What if that knowledge could guide them when they face situations similar to the ones their favorite heroes and villains have already faced?

> *Enter through the narrow gate. For wide is the gate and broad is the road that leads to destruction, and many enter through it. But small is the gate and narrow is the road that leads to life, and only a few find it.*
>
> *~ Matthew 7:13-14 ~*

Expanding the Paths for Guidance

Finally, as you'll see by the end of this book, I've come to believe that stories are one of the primary ways our Co-Author (my name for my creator — please feel free to use your own!) sends us clues and answers to help us with our current situations. While Aaron and I were organizing our thoughts for the book, we were amazed by the parallels between the themes of the stories we engaged during that time and the events that were transpiring in our lives. You truly just can't make that sh*t up.

And yet, it doesn't surprise me, as my professional life revolves around the power of story to connect us with each other, heal old wounds, and move forward into a truer personal and collective story. For the last decade, I've been blessed to help aspiring messengers (authors, speakers, coaches, and entrepreneurs) share their stories in a way that maximizes their impact on their audience, brand, and bottom line. Along the way, I witness them revisit and heal the old wounds that still exist in those stories.

A few years ago, I was able to articulate a pattern in the messenger journey that I believe will help you understand the depth of mindful awareness that we are talking about developing through interaction with Story.

Becoming the Co-Author of One's Story and Our Story

When I work with someone, the first step is understanding the big arc of the heroic story they want to share. They love that part. But then the work of writing in a deeply engaging way begins, and that's when they start wondering if they've made the biggest mistake of their life by hiring me. (It's true.)

I ask them to go back into their stories and write from *inside of the experience* — to bring the reader into the setting in which the story took place but also into the experience of the author's body, mind, and soul during those phases of their story. In other words, I ask them to *be the Character* in their story again, which inevitably means that they have to re-experience the pain (and joy) of the moments in their story. Over time, I've come to believe that this is necessary for both credibility (to make the reader certain that the author understands the reader's pain on all levels and build the trust necessary to continue reading and exploring their own healing journey), but also for the author's own healing. By revisiting the wounds with this level of intention, they uncover details of the story that crack open new awareness and let the light shine on (and heal) pain that was pushed into the dark recesses of their mind and body for survival.

They dive into their character and write through the pain with more awareness; and when they come up for air, my line of questioning to connect the dots of their story pulls them into *Narrator* awareness. They move from being inside of their story to looking at the whole of it from above, the same way the narrator of a book reports the extensive details that one character with only one perspective in a big story just cannot report. We connect some dots and then they dive back into *Character* awareness and then eventually into *Narrator* awareness again, and so on.

Near the end of their writing process, there is this moment where they are able to be both the *Character* and the *Narrator* at the same time. I know this has happened when they say something like, "No wonder I still have this issue (over here) in my life! Whenever _____ happens in my story, I always say/do _____!" They have found the moment where their character has had all the power to change the story but didn't know it. It's in that moment that they become a *Co-author* of their story — not just a *Character* that doesn't understand the themes of the bigger story they are in and feels at the mercy of other characters and plot-twists in the story, and not just the *Narrator* that understands the big themes but has no real power to change the story from inside of it. As a *Co-author*, they can experience moments from inside and outside them, and have access to all of that information to change the scripts and behaviors that keep them stuck in a painful story loop. They finish the book empowered to intentionally write the rest of their story the way they want it to go... as it unfolds.

But wouldn't it be amazing if they didn't have to suffer the decades of pain and go through this arduous process in order to develop these three levels of awareness and be the Co-author of their life?

Well, that's what I believe *A Religion of Story* makes possible for our children.

If we sit with them and bring their awareness to these three levels of awareness in the stories we engage, they can *practice these levels of awareness* and make it a habitual way of interacting with the characters and plot twists in their own lives. In other words, we can help them learn to be the human character and feel the impact of the story happening *to* them because we are human and designed to feel all of the pain and joy of life; and we can also help them learn how to see their own character in a larger context of the bigger story that is being written for their life and the world they naturally affect with their own words and choices. Most importantly, by guiding them to hold the tension of the Character and Narrator perspective, we can give them the opportunity to explore new choices in attitudes, words, and behaviors — the power to design their own life and contribute powerfully to a better collective story.

The Format of the Book

This book is a collaborative work so that you can see the experience from both the parent and the child's perspectives.

Amanda wrote the content that follows this image throughout the book.

In each of the chapters, which capture the themes of our favorite stories during that phase of our lives, we are inviting you to sit with us on our comfy couch (or recline with us on the big bed we made on the floor) and hang out with us during these conversations. You will see how deeper attention to the story arcs, characters, and messages, and how they related to *me*, sparked the discussions; and you'll probably laugh as you witness Aaron learning to get used to this — learning how to manage his frustration and eventually began to ask the questions before I did. (Note: While I was writing this, I wondered if I should encourage you to do it differently to prevent the frustration of interruptions; but I immediately knew that would be a mistake. Part of what I was doing when interrupting the story was teaching him to ask questions and be thoughtful *while watching it.* Eventually, he internalized my questions and began asking and answering them before I would even pause the show. He could be entertained without being entranced; he could learn from the stories and characters rather than blindly accepting the experiences and models he was watching.)

Following these stories, you will be invited to consider your own religion of story — *what* you actually believe about the theme at hand and *why* you believe it. To model this for you as part of my process of engaging Story with a child, I've given you a sneak peek into this mommy's psyche (consider yourself warned!) and my very own religion of story which was unconsciously shaped by all of the stories I watched, heard, and experienced in my formative years. Why? Well, as you read, by the time I had Aaron, I'd already become painfully aware that I had grown up absorbing the beliefs of those around me without so much as questioning whether they made sense. Because I was very clear that my religion of story had been shaped *without* my (or anyone else's) conscious awareness and intention, I knew there were assumptions and beliefs I had that simply were not true; and, as I engaged Aaron with Story, it was necessary for me to examine my reactions and what was driving them. If I didn't, I could have perpetuated the lies and impacted his capacity for more character and freedom.

Then you will have the opportunity to see the impact of this process on Aaron's life, from his perspective. If you are anything like our test readers, you'll laugh and cry and wonder if this level of self- and world-awareness is actually possible. When you do that, I want to invite you to expand that wondering to include your child and others: What would become possible for them as individuals, and for our culture as a whole,

Aaron wrote the content that follows this image throughout the book.

if they could walk through the world with this level of awareness, curiosity, and intention?

After my small personal wrap-up at the end of each chapter, Aaron and I have worked on "Deeper Dives" into the themes. This is our way of sharing some of the specific concepts we engaged around the theme in hopes that it will help to spark even more ideas for your discussions. For example, in Uncertainty, we used *Finding Nemo* characters to explore the various ways people react to the Unknown; and in Self-Knowledge, you'll see how you can use this

Amanda and Aaron co-wrote the content that follows this image throughout the book.

experience to learn more about your child's superpowers and kryptonite. Our goal isn't to give you questions to ask or tell you exactly how to do this; it's to give you enough of an idea of where you could take the discussions on each theme.

In other words, you'll see how the stories we were engaging on screen helped us make sense of the stories we were living, and you'll get the opportunity to dive deeper into the concepts we are exploring with the children and stories in your life.

Of course, as we were organizing the book, we quickly realized that Aaron's memories of the very early days are not as clear as mine, which is why we decided to format the book consistent with our level of engagement. In other words, in the beginning of the book, you'll be engaging more of my writing because I remember more of the conversations and was working out the way I was going to do this. However, you'll see the depth of Aaron's memory and writing start to expand as he gets older and owns his part in the experience with more and more intention. And, of course, he'll write the conclusion since that's what this is really all about anyway — raising a child in such a way that they can think, feel, and arrive at their own conclusions and navigate the world independently with strong character and a commitment to their own truth and freedom to maintain it. I can't wait to read his conclusions! I know he hasn't told me everything.

Before You Dive In

As we've begun writing this book, Aaron and I have had some big conversations about how to make the ideas accessible to parents and children from every background, which means that we've been imagining all of the possible objections and considering how we can navigate them.

But one thing I know because I'm a good two decades older than him is that it doesn't matter how hard we work (and we will); if we do a good job of presenting this new paradigm, it will necessarily upset parents for one or more reasons.

I mean, when I mentioned that my husband said a Nickelodeon cartoon was our family's bible, did you have a visceral reaction and immediately consider putting the book down? If you hail from a strong religious tradition with a sacred text, then that makes perfect sense. How about when I mentioned that we spend hours and hours in front of the tv together? If you have strong beliefs about technology and its impact on our culture and connections with each other, of course you questioned my approach. Or maybe you are one of those folks who loves to read books and detests the way they are developed for television or movies.

Whatever objections arise, I want to invite you to keep reading through all of the moments where the content makes you gasp a little. And it will. Sometimes, it will be a gasp of awe, but sometimes it will be a gasp of disbelief or judgment. Really, you're probably going to feel really judgy at least once or twice while you read, and I can almost predict where it will happen. I have watched a lot of very edgy tv series and movies with my kid, so edgy that even he has debated me about whether we should put them in the book or not. I am not personally afraid to be judged about this because I don't regret any of it. I'd do it again because I know that he's going to interact with stories full of violence, sexuality, and more throughout his life. I'm glad I was there, even though it was incredibly uncomfortable, to be a safe place for him to engage and process his way through his first experiences with these topics.

It's also important to say here that I am *not* a parenting expert or therapist, and that I'm not claiming that I have found *the only way* to cultivate character in a child and preserve freedom without dogma. That would be like throwing another bit of dogma out there for people to latch onto when the purpose of this book is to do exactly the opposite of that. I'm not trying to convert you. I don't have great answers to most of the questions I ask in the book.

One of my favorite professors in the honors program used to say, "If you have more answers than questions at the end of this program, we've failed you." And that's how I feel about this offering to the world.

Our hope is that, at the least, this cracks open a possibility for you to bring a little more mindfulness and intention to the experience of engaging stories with your family. And at the most, that you and your child enjoy some delicious conversations while you walk miles in other people's shoes and learn as much as you can before you step out of your living room and co-author your own stories.

Chapter One
Uncertainty

"Just keep swimming!"

~ Dori ~

"**M**ommy, I want to watch *Nemo*." His sweet little face looked up at me, pleading.

"Nemo? Again?" I smiled and shook my head, but just barely.

What is this? The thousandth time?!? I wondered silently.

"Yes!" he exclaimed as he skipped from the kitchen to the living room, expecting me to follow.

Well, I'm done with the dishes and totally exhausted. Maybe Nemo *is exactly what we both need.*

I dried my hands and dragged my achy body to the oversized living room where Aaron was already putting the disk into the DVD player.

"Okay, Mommy! Let's watch our show!" He pressed PLAY as he pulled himself onto the couch and snuggled into my side.

I do love this movie. Wounded, overprotective parent afraid of the big "bad" world damaging his son. I can totally relate.

I looked down at this treasure in my arms and thought about the declaration he'd made just the day before. We were driving home from the store and had stopped next to a school bus when his little voice chimed from the backseat, "Mommy, I'm ready for school!" I didn't feel ready for him to go to school, but I had promised to listen to him and the cues his soul had been giving me since he was born. I pulled him closer. *I'm not ready. But if you are — well, I guess we are going to find you a good preschool.*

While I understood the deep parental fear Marlin felt when Nemo was ready to explore, I'd made the decision to put my son's needs and desires ahead of my fears. Through my experience helping to raise little ones and my education in child development, I knew that ignoring a child's need for novelty and squashing their curiosity with overly-strict boundaries was a recipe for never-ending power struggles. Plus, I'd learned about the power of self-image, words, and expectation — how children rise (or fall) to the level of an influential adult's expectations. So, instead of telling my son not to go out into the deep waters because "the ocean isn't safe," I had decided I would go with him into those uncomfortable unknowns and support him because… unknowns create uncertainty, and it's awful to face uncertainty alone. I'd also determined to be the voice of courage and truth in his life, even if it didn't come naturally, because we lived with someone who addressed all of his curiosity and adventurous behavior with, "You're gonna break your neck!" I knew that in order for him to grow into a confident, responsible adult, he needed to be trusted and then carefully guided through all of the unknowns he would face while growing up.

In order to become more than we are, we have to expand into unknown territory and master it… and I promised to be with him on the journey, I thought as I tucked the blanket around us, knowing he would stay riveted to the screen while I drifted into naptime.

"Aaron, how did Nemo feel about going to school?" I asked when the movie was over.

"He's excited!" he exclaimed, his fists clenched and up in demonstration of the emotion. Then he dropped them, "But his dad's *not* excited."

"Why do you think he's not excited?" I probed.

"I don't know." He shrugged his shoulders.

"Well, what happened to Nemo's mom?" I looked straight into his eyes.

"She got eaten by a big fish." His voice was matter-of-fact and a little sad as he remembered that terrible moment at the beginning of the movie.

"Right, so Nemo's dad probably feels..." I let the sentence stem hang for him to finish.

"Scared?" He turned to me with eyebrows raised in emerging awareness.

"Exactly. Mommies and daddies know that sometimes, when we try new things, we get disappointed or even hurt. But that's why you kids are so cool. You just go out and try it. You don't let being scared stop you. That's why we have to work together, Aaron. You can go out and try new things, like going to school, and your mommy and daddy will be here to help you."

"Ohhh..."

"Yeah, *I* feel like Nemo's dad today. A little nervous because I've never had a little boy go to school."

"You're scared?"

"Well, sure. But that's just because like Nemo's dad, I want to protect you from growing pains. But I can't. That's how you're going to learn. So I'm just gonna be here to help you when you go out and do something new and find that it's harder than you thought it would be. Okay?"

"Okay, Mommy." He patted my hand and went to play with his toys — a cue that he was "full up" with adult talk and needed time to process.

I don't know how much of that he understood, but I hope he felt my heart — that I'll always be with him to help him through any uncertainties he shares with me.

Uncertainty

What did you learn about uncertainty from your favorite childhood movies, tv series, and books? Did the characters choose the unknown, or were they thrust into it? Were they excited about a wild and crazy adventure, or were they terrified to leave home and try anything new? Did they have one reaction initially and then feel differently after they took a few steps? Were they rewarded for their journey into unknown territories, or were they met with so many obstacles that they (and you) wondered if it was worth it for them to leave home at all?

When I was little, the two characters I interacted with the most, Dorothy from Wizard of Oz and Elliott from E.T., were just going along their merry way when the Unknown came a swirlin' in their direction. Neither one of them really asked for their lives to be turned upside-down, but they were. I remember feeling absolutely riveted, compelled to finish the movies, despite the many ugly witch cackles, terrifying flying monkeys, and misty-night jump-scares.

Of course, not too long after these films, I was introduced to Ariel (*The Little Mermaid*) whose curiosity drew her to uncharted waters. From her story, I learned that even when you choose the unknown and walk into uncertainty, challenges await. Oh, and there are dark forces just waiting for you to take that one misstep, so they can trap or exploit you and your superpowers for their dark purposes. Sure, love always wins, but damn — that's a scary journey! Is it worth it?

And then there was Ray (*Field of Dreams*) who was gently invited into the unknown by a whisper on the wind: "Build it and they will come." From him, I learned that even when we are on a supernaturally-supported path, we will be faced with big doses of self-doubt that will regularly be induced by others thinking we are absolutely nuts for taking such big risks "with no physical evidence to support the hunch."

Now that you have identified some of the patterns in your early exposure to uncertainty, do you see any commonalities between the experiences of uncertainty you watched in stories and those that have appeared in your own life?

Well, it doesn't take a rocket scientist to look at my history and see the impact of these stories on my life.

I grew up in a home with a dad much like Nemo's. He had suffered so much trauma and pain in his childhood that he found it nearly impossible to imagine, let alone experience, his children dealing with any pain at all. Just like Nemo,

I was encouraged to stay close to his side and avoid all unnecessary risks. And that's what I did. I lived a small, quiet, and sheltered life, protected by my father, mother, and the extended family we developed in our small town. And boy, was I protected! From *all* potentially dangerous activities, people, perspectives, and beliefs.

The problem was that they couldn't protect me from everything, and they couldn't protect me forever. When I did experience uncertainty in my situations at school or with friends, my big-little-girl feelings and fears were sometimes too big, too inconvenient, or too distressing for them to let me feel; and I learned to push all of those down, down, down so as not to burden the people I loved. Instead, I tried to just stay on the narrow yellow brick road put in front of me and avoid everything beyond its borders, including the feelings I carefully placed outside of it. Without all of that emotion getting in the way, I became a super high-performing and responsible student and daughter. In fact, I was so focused on staying on the path and doing all the right things to keep myself and everyone else safe that I lost access to my childhood curiosity and desires. I was making do with my known, ordinary world; and I didn't think twice about it until I got to the university.

At eighteen years old, I nearly drowned in the Unknown. Separated from my biological and religious families, I found myself alone, nurturing a new relationship with my high-school-soulmate and engaging big questions for which I was completely unprepared: Is God real? How do I know that? How on God's Earth am I supposed to read all of these books, understand and discuss them, and deal with the hot mess of fear raging inside my mind and body? Having learned early how to push that annoying emotion out of my way, I doubled-down on my ability to focus and perform in spite of it. And over-perform I did. I had everyone fooled, actually. Straight A's. A degree in Social Science with Secondary Education. Graduating with honors. Completing a thesis project in which I helped others train their mind to overcome physical, mental, and emotional challenges. Completing all of the requirements for my teaching credential.

That's when I had Aaron. And let me tell you — of all of the unknowns I've ever experienced, I have never found a more terrifying unknown than that of motherhood. And I *knew* how to take care of babies after helping to care for my two much-younger sisters! I just had no idea how to raise a child to be happier and healthier than I was, and I had no one I trusted to help me figure that out.

All of the above unknowns were like Dorothy's and Elliott's — thrust upon me.

But by the time I was having this conversation with Aaron about Nemo, I was stepping into another version of Unknown: entrepreneurship. When he went to school, my part-time work as an online writing instructor quickly shifted to full-service editing and content development for a group of small entrepreneurs, and I was being asked to think bigger and bigger than I ever had.

We were stepping into the next Unknown together, both of us choosing it. But I was scared and he wasn't. In fact, the night before I took my first big step in business, when my anxiety was taking over, I asked: "Aaron, if you had a friend who was going to school for the first time and feeling really nervous about it, what would you say to encourage him?" He smiled and put his hand on my face, as if he knew that I was asking for myself: "Be brave. Use your imagination. And ask for help."

When Everything Changes

Under the bright light of our living room game table, I looked at my hand of cards menacingly. I knew something that nobody else did, and I could feel that I was going to destroy them all.

The game was Uno and if you've never heard of it—first of all, do you live under a rock? And second, all you need to know for now is that the goal of the game is to get rid of all of your cards. The first person to do so wins.

So, five-year-old me was sitting there with my mom, dad, and great-grandma, barely tall enough to get my elbows on the table, with a sly look stretched across my baby face.

It was my turn.

In my hand, I held a wild card which, if played, would make the person to my left draw four cards and set them so far back in the game that there would be little hope of them winning.

It was time. I raised my eyebrows and reached my empty hand out, pulling the wild card out of my tiny grip, and placing it onto the stack of cards in the middle of the table. Everyone gasped, only fueling my overwhelming desire to be the one true champion of this game. (Oh yes, I was very competitive.)

To my left was my mom, who studied her hand intently. She only had a few cards, meaning she was really close to winning the game. It was perfect. The stars were aligning! There was no way she would come back from this.

She raised her eyebrows, seemingly unmoved by my power play. Slowly and confidently, she reached for her cards and played another wild card on top of mine!

Everyone ooohed, my Dad grimacing because he now had to draw eight cards instead of four.

"Bahahaha!!! Oh, man! Too bad," I said with an extraordinary amount of glee. Even though Mom was still close to winning, I was still very much in the game. And besides, it's always great seeing someone get absolutely pummeled by an unexpected eight-card draw. Our attention turned to Dad, whose reaction rapidly turned from displeasure to cheer. The anticipation built as he pulled a card from his hand and threw it onto the table.

"NO WAY!"

"Oh, no!"

"Whaaaaaat..."

That's right, he stacked yet another wild card! This was incredible and quite an uncommon event in Uno. Now, my great-grandma would have to draw not four, not eight, but twelve cards. She was so screwed, and I was elated!

"Ooo, Grandma. You have to draw twelve cards!"

Oh, but my elation was short-lived. I don't know how to describe it, but I had this feeling, this... dreadful shadow fell over me. My great-grandma started reaching for a card, and

I knew that there was something wrong. Her face said it all: There was nothing that could stop what was coming.

I couldn't believe this was happening. With such confidence and grace, my great-grandma slapped down a fourth wild card.

My mouth hung agape. My heart pounded. My eyes welled.

I looked around at everyone, dead silent. They stared at me, unsure of how I was going to react. At this age, I hadn't yet learned how to lose with dignity and be a good sport.

My chin quivered until I couldn't hold back the streams of tears that began to pour down my face. I cried, and I cried, and I cried. Having to draw sixteen cards was too much for my five-year-old ego to bear.

"That's not fair..." I cried. Everyone was sad to see me so upset, but the writing was on the wall. I would have to pick up all those cards whether I liked it or not. It was either that, or I would have to forfeit the game.

Slowly, I picked up my cards, one by one. I was doomed. There's no way I will win the game, I thought. My small hands couldn't even hold all of those cards.

My tears started to fade, but the pain just got worse. Card after card, my hand grew, crushing all hope of victory... or did it?

As I pulled the cards, blinking through my tears, I started to realize something... something hopeful. The cards I picked were really good cards, many of them being wild cards and "draw-two's," which would help me make the next person draw two cards instead of four. But it was just as exciting.

I studied my hand intently, organizing it in the methodical way that I do. I smiled... and then I smiled more. "I'm going to destroy you all!"

Even though I still ended up losing that game, I gleaned an important lesson. Just when we think we're about to kill it, everything can fall apart. It happens, and often with bigger consequences than having to draw sixteen cards (which really sucks too, don't get me wrong).

Being able to stay strong, look for the silver lining, and adapt in the face of uncertainty is crucial; and if we can hold steady, our recovery will be so much sweeter and we're bound to learn an important lesson along the way.

We see this in our favorite stories, too. Dorothy *(Wizard of Oz)* was whirled out of Kansas and dropped into Oz. Although she was scared, she had no choice but to find a way home. And in the end, she learned that she had the power within herself to change her reality all along.

Marlin *(Finding Nemo)* was deadly afraid of the ocean outside of his anemone. He forbade Nemo from leaving because he saw the "outside world" was too dangerous and full of uncertainties. But, when Nemo ran away from home, Marlin pushed through his own limits to save his son. He later understood that the world beyond wasn't so bad, and that it was his job to guide Nemo through the uncertainties of life.

And just as Marlin didn't want to leave his home, I too did not want to leave mine.

In the Summer of 2016, my family and I moved from the home where I was born and raised in Southern California to

Portland, Oregon. Never before had we been on our own and so far from our favorite people.

I was thirteen at the time and about to transition to eighth grade. Now that I look back on it, we really had no idea what we were doing. Like, seriously. No idea. And now that I'm older, I realize this is a normal thing that adults experience, so that's cool, I guess.

I made my resistance to the idea of moving clear, yet I knew it was the next right step for us. Oregon had more trees, more hills, and more green, but it was barren of familiarity, family, and friends. My entire life story up to that point was written in my childhood home, and the thought of starting a new chapter was entirely alien to me.

I felt like Bilbo Baggins *(The Hobbit)*, safe in my little bubble. I had never moved before and enjoyed the luxuries of our situation. I mean, I even had a pool. Why would I want to leave? But somewhere inside me, I knew there was something more out there for us and was called to the possibilities of starting over and taking a risk. Just like Bilbo, I felt an inexplicable pull to the unknown and the adventure that was waiting for me.

We had a stressful trek up north, but a comforting destination awaited us.

Our new home was amazing. It was spacious. I had a nice room and an amazing backyard (with a trampoline!) and I quickly became too comfortable in my new bubble. After dealing with a lot of uncertainty with the move, it felt nice not having to face so much of it. I began online school (which totally sucked) and slowly guarded myself from new experiences. I had no friends and I didn't have anything to do that "lit me up" inside, nothing to "stretch" me and introduce me to uncomfortable situations (in healthy doses, of course).

And now that I think about it, my hostility toward uncertainty was so odd for me—a complete one-eighty from how I was in my earlier years. I was a curious rebel (just like my whole damn family—go figure!) and one of those kids that was frequently told, "Stop that! Get down from there! You're gonna break your neck!"

But here, in this new bubble, I was so inflexible and opposed to experiencing newness that I regularly got frustrated when asked if I wanted to take a walk outside with my parents. I was safe in my room with my normal routine, not having to leave my comfort zone.

It was almost like I was Chihiro *(Spirited Away)* and every time something new and scary happened, I ran away and tried to forget. And if that didn't work, I fought it at every turn. No, my parents were never turned into pigs like Chihiro's—thank God!—but I had my fair share of opportunities that were presented to me and I turned them down without consideration, either out of habit or insecurity, and I always played it "safe."

Around this time, I became obsessed with the movie Howl's Moving Castle which is all about facing our internal (and in many cases, external) demons. It taught me that I shouldn't run away from my fears and the scary stuff that life tends to throw our way. Either we make the decision to face the uncertainty or it festers and morphs, oftentimes into something beyond our control.

Thankfully, after my terrible online education experience, I insisted that it was time for something new.

One year later, I walked into my first improv comedy class. I had always been interested in trying improv, especially after watching *Whose Line Is It Anyway?* for the first time, and I decided to jump in when the opportunity presented itself.

I was expecting nothing, but I came with an open attitude. Keep in mind that this was my first time going to physical school since California. I was still fairly inflexible and resistant when it came to new things, but something about this was different.

Improv is a type of theater where you make everything up on the spot. There's no preparation or rehearsal—just jump in, don't overthink things (whaaaat?), and have fun.

So, basically what I'm saying is that improv is a sport where you're constantly confronting the unknown. Go figure.

What do I do or say next?

Should it be something funny or serious?

Oh no, how do I even respond to that?

But as I practiced, I started to realize that there's always a way to take any situation and turn it into something even better.

One of the first concepts I learned in improv is to "Yes, and"—to accept whatever "offer" I was given by my scene partner(s) like a statement, an action, etc.—and build upon it. Denying an offer is something that rarely happens, and it can throw a whole scene out of whack.

Not only was I constantly confronting the unknown, I was also learning how to be flexible. I needed to give up control, get out of my comfort zone, and stop trying to be perfect.

Again, GO FIGURE.

My improv instructor liked to remind us that, "Perfection is the enemy of the good." You can imagine my brain sputtering after I heard that for the first time. I had to learn to be okay with failure. In fact, failure is encouraged in improv. Failure can be comical, sure; but more importantly, it opens up more opportunities in a scene (and in life, wink wink) for growth and redemption.

Learning to be okay with the unknown and the constant threat of falling flat on our face is probably one of the best things anyone can learn—especially when there are serious consequences for our actions.

At the time of writing, COVID-19 is finally ending (knock on wood). It's been over a year of perpetual uncertainty for the world on a level not seen for a long time. So, you know what life decided to throw at me? A new business, graduation, several mock trial competitions, and a 1,200-mile move... because why not?!

Right.

But you know what? I'm ready for it. I've learned to trust the uncertainty, and I know the reward for facing it is almost always something better at the end... even if it doesn't feel that way at first.

I might even dare to say that I willingly look for uncertainty at times, just as the brave souls on the Starship Enterprise *(Star Trek)* had. After all, nobody ever said that exploring brave new worlds would be easy.

What If We Could Learn to Love The Unknown, or At Least Not Hate It?

It's been about nine months since Aaron and I started this book project, and the timing of me working on the wrap-ups of the chapters is just hilarious to me. (You'll have to catch us on an interview to hear about the collaborative process and how we started in the middle, skipped certain chapters, changed formats a few times, and such.) Aaron turned eighteen a few months ago, and I find myself circling back to the same feelings and even experiences I had that day we watched *Nemo* so many years ago.

My son is an adult — a man — and I've never had an adult son before. Plus, that business I started all those years ago has turned into something quite magical and is expanding quickly this year as Aaron and my sister and a few of my clients-turned-friends are now becoming team members. We're launching a podcast and new offerings, working on another collaborative book, and... well, there are so many unknowns. And of course, you saw that we are making a big move.

Uncertainty has found its way into every corner of my life this year and it has upped the ante. *How do I navigate this new iteration of my relationship with my son? Am I really capable of being the type of leader that this company and our clients need? How in the world do I work with family and maintain healthy boundaries? Where are we going to be living and how will our lives change? Am I really ready to have an empty nest?* Gulp.

Fortunately, I've been here before and I at least know *not* to run away, even when everything in my body and mind is screaming for me to do just that. After decades of navigating uncertainty, a little better with every round, I've learned a few tricks that help me and everyone else around me skip a little more down that yellow brick road to... wait, where are we headed? Ah, who cares! Let's hold hands and go!

Diving Deeper into Uncertainty
with Your Kids and Their Stories

Default Reactions to Uncertainty

There are a variety of ways that people react when confronted with uncertainty, and a lot of it is rooted in our "animal" instincts or, as many refer to it, our "reptilian and mammalian brains." Our minds often perceive great uncertainty as a physical or psychological threat, which can trigger those "animal" responses like fight, flight, or freeze.

While these reactions can be helpful for surviving true danger (who knows, maybe I'll need to run from a bear one day), they can also be counterproductive when we are not facing anything more than simple uncertainty.

Imagine how much more confident and powerful your child could be in the face of uncertainty with a deeper understanding of what their favorite characters are experiencing (and what we all experience) in the body and mind at an unconscious level.

Fight

One reaction to uncertainty is to mobilize or to fight our way through our current circumstance. We do this when we think we can overcome whatever challenge we meet.

When threatened with the possibility of being hurt by the cruel human girl, Gill *(Finding Nemo)* tried to fight his way out of the fish tank and rescue his friends, too. Fighting their way to freedom appeared to be the only way out of their uncertain and high-stakes future.

Of course, Dorothy *(Wizard of Oz)* was whirled out of Kansas and dropped into Oz. Although she was scared, she had no choice but to mobilize herself and others to find a way home.

And then there was Katniss *(The Hunger Games)*, who volunteered her life for her little sister when she was chosen to fight — and almost certainly die — in the Hunger Games. She fought to protect her sister and her family by sacrificing herself for them.

Which of your favorite characters have decided to fight back when faced with uncertainty?

Flee or Freeze

Confronting the unknown feels like too much at times, leading many to run away. And when the going gets tough and it seems like there's nowhere to run, and no way to win, we freeze, play dead, and hope for the best.

After being turned into an old woman by the Wicked Witch of the Waste, Sophie *(Howl's Moving Castle)* ran away to seek Howl's assistance in removing her curse.

Marlin's *(Finding Nemo)* response to Nemo wanting to leave their anemone was to freeze and insist his son do the same. He forbade Nemo from leaving their anemone because he saw the "outside world" was too dangerous and full of uncertainties.

When Aang *(Avatar: The Last Airbender)* found out he was the Avatar, he fled from the air temple, rejected his obligation, ran away, and was caught in a harsh storm. Then, he "froze" himself (yes, literally) in an iceberg to protect himself from dying at sea.

Which of your favorite characters have either run away, or been paralyzed with fear (at least for some time) when faced with uncertainty?

Follow Curiosity

Not everyone responds to uncertainty by running away, freezing in place, or fighting through it. In fact, sometimes curiosity is in the driver's seat and we feel that we need to run *toward* uncertainty rather than away from it. Children tend to do this more naturally because they don't have as much exposure to danger or experience with its results.

Obviously, Nemo *(Finding Nemo)* wanted to leave his anemone, go to school, and learn about the outside world. Those on the Starship Enterprise (*Star Trek: The Next Generation*) were determined "to explore strange new worlds; to seek out new life and new civilizations; to boldly go where no man has gone before."

Even Charlie *(All Dogs Go to Heaven 2)* left heaven because it lacked novelty and excitement, and he loved getting into trouble too much to stay.

Which of your favorite characters have used curiosity to navigate uncertain moments, challenges, or adventures?

Go with the Flow

You know those people that just go with the flow? It's an interesting way of responding to uncertainty, and you know what? Sometimes we just need to stop worrying about the uncertainty and allow life to take us where we need to go.

Crush (*Finding Nemo*) the sea turtle was a great example of this as he let the East Australian Current guide his way through the ocean. He and his other sea turtle friends were quite literally "going with the flow."

At first, Bilbo Baggins *(The Hobbit)* was reluctant to join Gandalf the dwarves on their quest, but decided to go with them at the last minute. He wasn't particularly adventurous and he definitely didn't know what to expect — he was along for the ride.

Someone we loved dearly used to say that used to say that there are three kinds of people in this world: People who make things happen, people who watch things happen, and people who don't know what the hell just happened. And when it comes to going with the flow, Dori *(Finding Nemo)* definitely jives with the latter. Of course, the short-term memory probably helped at least a little bit!

*Which of your favorite characters have a
go-with-the-flow approach to uncertainty?*

New Responses
Every hero will eventually be confronted with uncertainty,
but what's important is how they choose to respond to it...
eventually. Their initial responses are often reactionary and
imperfect, but the journey through that uncertainty usually
sparks bravery and an understanding so great that it allows
the hero to respond in an appropriate way — to consciously
choose how to respond rather than always letting their
"animal brain" take over.

Marlin *(Finding Nemo)* willingly swam into the unknown,
nearly dying multiple times, so he could save his son. The story
concluded with a new understanding that while the unknown
can be dangerous and frightening, it's a necessary part of life.
It's better to embrace it than to ignore it.

After being broken out of his iceberg, Aang *(Avatar: The
Last Airbender)* realized that he had turned his back on the
world. He came to terms with his obligation to the four nations
and decided to fight back against the Fire Nation rather than
run away from his duty as the Avatar. He became a fighter, but
a mindful one that responded to each situation accordingly.
The one time he didn't respond mindfully, he suffered big
consequences that reminded him of the importance of
choosing the right action at the right time.

Instead of being a victim of life's unforeseen
circumstances — most notably, being transported to a strange
land via a tornado — Dorothy *(The Wizard of Oz)* accrued allies
and defeated the Witch of the West once and for all.

Sophie *(Howl's Moving Castle)* fled to Howl's castle,
hoping that he could remove her curse; but after her
interactions with Howl, she quickly realized that we can't
run away from our problems — we need to face our demons
or they will fester. She stood up, dealt with unknown worlds

and people, and searched for the truth — all while helping Howl face his demons, too.

Following his first unexpected adventure throughout Middle Earth in The Hobbit, Bilbo *(The Lord of the Rings)* reluctantly accepted his uncertain future after turning over his ring and decided to embark on an adventure of his own to Rivendell.

By being aware of how we react to uncertainty, we can make the conscious decision to respond in whatever way is appropriate — whether that be to fight, to flee, to freeze, to be curious, to go with the flow, or otherwise. We can choose to become the master of uncertainty rather than let uncertainty be the master of us.

*Which of these reactions are your typical
response to uncertainty?*

Does it depend on the type of uncertainty you are facing?

*How about your child?
What is their typical response?*

*How can you help them understand that these are natural
responses, like their favorite heroes and villains have,
and that it's what they do with them that cultivates their
character (or not) or leads to their freedom (or not)?*

When children know how to navigate uncertainty and fear by regulating their nervous system response, they have more opportunities to develop resilience. Of course, the happy byproduct of this level of self-awareness is that they also become harder to control through intimidation and fear, which means less bullying, more confidence, and the ability to preserve freedom for themselves and others.

Chapter Two
Self-Knowledge

"Yay, you failed! And it was awesome!
Exceptional! Outstanding!"

~ Meet The Robinsons ~

I wiped the tears away while Aaron watched the whole Robinson family congratulate little Lewis on his failure, which had resulted in a huge mess. Furniture and family members were all covered in peanut butter and jelly. Taking a deep breath to soothe the ache in my chest, I shook my head at how deeply this scene affected me.

I still feel like I can't make a mistake without making everyone in my world upset with me forever. I looked over at him, feeling grateful that we were watching a movie with a message that "failure is a necessary part of learning" and that we need to "keep moving forward." *I don't know how I'm going to change this experience for myself, but I'll be damned if I'm gonna make him feel like he can't make a mistake without losing his sense of belonging.*

He didn't notice my quiet, tear-streaked observation of his sweet little face.

Well, I guess we're on the right track based on today's exchange. I stifled a giggle as I remembered what had transpired when he'd walked into the dining room where I was working on my laptop.

"Mom, am I about to get into trouble?" he'd asked.

I'd looked up from my laptop computer into the concerned face of my five-year-old. "What makes you think you're going to get into trouble?" I probed.

"You have that look on your face," he'd stated matter-of-factly.

"What look is that?" I'd pushed.

"This one…" and he'd cocked his head to the side and adjusted his eyebrows to mirror mine. It was definitely an "I caught you" expression.

Omg, that's so funny.

"Did you do something wrong?" I'd asked, suppressing a smile again.

"No, that's why I'm confused," he'd offered.

"I'm upset with this person who sent me this email and their shenanigans. That look wasn't for you, but thanks for checking." I'd motioned him to come around the table for a hug before he'd headed outside to play.

I love that he's sensitive to expressions, but I'm especially happy that he asks about them. When I was his age, I always assumed the upset faces in my home and school were my fault, and I felt powerless to change it. Like I was breaking rules or failing people I loved, but had no idea which rule or how to stop failing them. Who am I kidding? I still feel that way sometimes.

As he watched little Lewis's surprise at the enthusiastic reaction to his failure, I thought about how hard I'd worked to change this story with him. I'd made a very clear distinction between his essential worth and lovability, and his choices and actions.

That day he clarified the distinction for Gramma with, "I'm not a bad boy... I just made a bad choice... and I'm sorry," was evidence that his storyline will not follow mine exactly, but I still have to be careful with my own responses, especially when I'm disciplining him.

I smiled again as I thought about the last time I'd caught him lying. I didn't want to push my fears on him or make a statement about his character, but I didn't know how else to handle it. After a talk with his dad, I'd decided to acknowledge his cleverness as a strength but explain that there were appropriate and inappropriate uses of it: "Hey, someday, all of this amazing storytelling ability you have is going to be really useful. Today, it's going to get you into trouble because we expect you to tell the truth around here."

That definitely worked, I surmised as I turned my whole body to face him and he turned the tv off. I was ready with my question for the day. "Aaron, what do you think Lewis learned by the end of this movie?"

"Keep moving forward!" he exclaimed, hands up in the air in declaration.

"Yes, and...?"

"Ughhh... Mom... why do you always ask me these questions?!?" His exasperation was real.

"Because the answers are important, Aaron."

He caught himself half-way through an eyeroll and settled against the couch for the conversation.

"When Lewis failed in the beginning of the movie, how did he feel?" I asked.

"Bad. He looked really sad and worried," Aaron answered, still exasperated.

"Right, it kinda looked like he wasn't sure if he would ever get it right. But then how about at the end of the movie?" I asked.

"Well, the Robinsons cheered when he failed, so I think he felt better about it."

"Right. They were all scientists or inventors themselves and knew that to build anything, you have to try and fail and try and fail and try again until you get it right."

"Makes sense." He nodded.

"It reminds me of how you changed your thinking the other night with the Uno game."

"Which one?" he asked, head cocked to the side.

"You know, the one where you thought you had us whooped?"

"Oh yeah..." He scrunched his nose and looked down at his hands and then smiled widely. He knew he'd figured something out that night.

Self-Knowledge

What did you learn about success and failure from your favorite childhood movies, tv series, and books, and what do those discoveries indicate about who you are? Did the heroes know their superpower that made them capable of achieving their goal, or did they discover it along the journey? Did they lose access to their superpower and have to remember or reclaim it? Did your heroes succeed quickly and easily, or did they struggle against external or internal villains? Did they face self-doubt, fears, and failures? Did they wonder if they "had the stuff" to stay the course?

When I think about the stories I was engaging during my early childhood, I see characters who didn't set out to be heroes and who didn't really see themselves as "special" in any way. They were simply thrust into the Unknown and onto the path of Self-Knowledge (and self-acceptance). Two of them — Dorothy *(Wizard of Oz)* and Atreyu *(Neverending Story)* — were given physical objects to help or protect them on their journeys. Those ruby red slippers and that medallion were believed to be the source of their power or protection; but by the end of the stories, we see that they "had the power [within them] all along." Their journey led them to discovering who they really were and that their true power was inside of them. Then there was Ren *(Footloose)*, whose superpowers were his desire to dance and share the experience with everyone else, and the curiosity and compassion that helped him understand his antagonists and eventually build a bridge of understanding and acceptance. And, of course, we cannot leave out Belle *(Beauty and The Beast)*. Belle, the girl with her head stuck in books, was forced to embody all of the qualities of curiosity, bravery, and true love that were merely ideals and imaginations up 'til then.

The Beast, on the other hand, had to tame his beastly self and let someone see the good in him that he had long-forgotten.

As I refamiliarized myself with these stories to prepare for this book, I was struck by the mirrors in my own life. Like Dorothy and Atreyu, well-intentioned people gave me external objects, symbols, and people, and called them my source of power and salvation. And unlike Ren, I just accepted the status quo and followed the traditions, even when they terrified me or made no sense. It wasn't until I had to follow in Belle's footsteps, to save a beloved family member from an unacceptable fate, that I had the opportunity to uncover my own superpowers and embody the qualities of my childhood heroes.

When Aaron and I were talking about Lewis and the importance and value of failure, I was taking very cautious steps forward in my business. I loved the projects that crossed my desk, but I wasn't exactly putting myself and my services out there in any big way because I was new to the game and doubting my ability to survive as an entrepreneur. Truthfully, I was doubting everything, including my superpowers.

In fact, even after my mentor asked me to edit her book and applauded my work, all I could do was ask her how it felt to know that her readers were going to be different people by the time they finished her book. In true mentor fashion, she cocked her head to the side and said, "It feels amazing, Amanda. When are you going to write your book?" Immediately, all of my insecurities choked me. This brilliant woman was telling me that she believed I was capable of writing a book and impacting readers, and all I could see in myself was a failure and a fraud. Behind the smile and the high-performer productivity, I was hiding a whole lot of fear, pain, and hopelessness. When I gave her a snarky deflective response about writing a book that she could put her name on, she firmly pushed back: "Amanda, you have something of value to give to the world today. What is it?" Unequipped to manage the emotions that were choking me, I said a quick goodbye, ran to my car, burst into tears, and started the long drive home, asking myself the question: "What value do I have to give the world today?"

About half-way home, I got my answer in the form of a memory of that moment when Aaron had corrected his angry great-grandmother: "I'm not bad. I made a bad choice and I'm sorry." That moment was the culmination of all of the lessons I'd acquired as the eldest child; a student of the classics, the subconscious, and the educational process; and as a classroom and online instructor. I knew the power of the mind and emotions, and I was doing everything I could with messages to raise a happy, healthy, thoughtful human being. As I remembered that moment with pride, I had access to true self-knowledge. I could see all of the value that I brought to this world and how it had been cultivated over the course of my lifetime so that I could help other moms avoid the pitfalls of generational disempowerment. By the time I got home, I was ready to work on the outlines for a series of parent/children books and download the bigger vision. Literally, it was like I stepped into a parallel universe. In the one I was living in when my mentor asked me the question, I had no access to what I've come to call "my magic egg" — the innate worth and wisdom I am here to share with the world.

Thirty minutes later, I could see it and had a plan for how to share it with others. Vital energy surged through me for the first time in my life.

With that glimpse of my "magic egg," I remembered I was made for more than the tired, powerless life I was living. Three months later, after much attention and action, I found myself in the world of transformational facilitation and an opportunity to deepen my self-knowledge. It was true that I am a powerful human being who is destined to impact the world; but it was also true that I had to face old st*ries, pain, and parts of my humanity that I had been pushing down and away for two decades. It was in that community that I experienced the power, beauty, and impact of fully embracing all of me — my divinity (magic egg) and my humanity (pain, st*ries, flaws, etc.). It was the beginning of my journey back to me — the reclamation and embodiment of everything that makes me magical and messy. That journey continues today through my work in the world, and especially through my motherhood journey.

Aaron and I have had hundreds of conversations about the importance of knowing oneself deeply — understanding how we work as humans in general and the power that we have to change our st*ries, the importance of owning and cultivating our magic eggs, and the necessity of embracing the incomplete or hurting parts of us that need love and acceptance. And I've been able to use our religion of story to see more of who he is and nurture it.

Getting to Know and Own Me

It was that time of the year again — "Back to School" season — also commonly known as every kid's least favorite time of the year.

You're tortured for a whole month with the knowledge that summer is almost over. You feel the seconds tick by as you're assaulted by seemingly never-ending school supplies commercials. And perhaps worst of all, you're forced to choose your extracurriculars for the next year, essentially forcing you to dig your own grave.

I know, I'm a drama king. But that's how it felt the summer before I was sitting at my school's orientation with my mom to my right and my dad to hers. The principal was on the large stage that towered in the auditorium speaking about the year ahead.

In my hands, I held the orientation packet that we grabbed on our way inside. Staring at its glossy plastic cover, I flipped open the pages and started browsing.

A message from the principal… New staff… Lunch program… Oh, no — Extracurriculars.

Before I had the chance to escape and flip to the next section, my mom peeked over and saw where I landed. Of course, it was the page where the school play was boldly advertised. *Crap.*

"Ohhhhh, are you going to do theatre this year?!" my mom asked quietly with an irritating amount of enthusiasm.

Not again…

Obviously displeased, I replied (probably with an eye-roll), "No, Mom, I'm not."

"Come on, you're so good at it. I still remember how much you loved shaking your ass up on stage when you went to Montessori." Her tone was pleading.

I hate it when she says that.

My stomach churned, and my cheeks reddened. I felt like Aang (*Avatar: The Last Airbender*), being told who I was meant to be and rejecting part of my calling (even though I wasn't being asked to defeat the Fire Lord and bring balance to the whole world). I knew it was true, but I refused to admit it.

"Oh my God, Mom. Stop it!" Visions of my time on the grand graduation stage at my old school flashed before me. I remembered it vividly... I definitely had fun, but...

"Why don't you want to do it?" she probed.

"I... I don't know. I just don't want to, okay?" I was clearly frustrated, but even *I* had no idea why.

My mom crooked her mouth to one side and looked at me lovingly, respecting my resistance. I felt bad for getting as upset and defensive as I did, but I didn't dig deeper. I never asked myself "Why?" Never allowed myself to be curious. Never acknowledged my past feelings about performing. Just decided to never do it.

Somewhere along the way, I had started to think that performing was somehow embarrassing and that I wasn't good at it. I decided to swear it off for good.

I think my mom probably looked at me and saw Lewis (*Meet The Robinsons*), a kid who expressed his incredible inventive and mechanical genius until he made a mistake.

At the moment that it mattered, his invention fell apart in front of his whole school. This, of course, led him to feeling irritated whenever his history of inventing was brought up.

Or maybe I was more like Molly (*Mr. Magorium's Wonder Emporium*) who was a natural at managing the Emporium; but when the time came for her to take ownership of the business, she lost belief in herself. Everyone around Molly could see her talent and passion so clearly—just like my mom saw mine—and yet, she was utterly blind to her own genius. She repeatedly turned the opportunity away until she finally allowed herself to be open to the possibility that she could do it.

As I got older, I lost sight of how fun performing was for me and my belief in myself. I never chose to experience again what it's like to step into the spotlight and forget to breathe. I never felt what it was like to screw up in front of everybody, but walk away knowing that I gave it my all. I never knew the sweet relief and the pride of putting on my best performance. No opportunity for risk-taking. No opportunity for courage. It was just me, behind the walls of my unexplained insecurities, inside the shell of my past.

That was before high school changed everything.

Exiting eighth grade, I had dealt with my least favorite schooling situation ever. We had just moved to Oregon and, uh... well, we aren't *big fans* of the public education system, so we decided to do online public homeschooling while we searched for something better. We thought, you know, it would probably be better than in-person public schooling at least.

It wasn't.

I was met with curriculum and requirements that seemed absurd, requiring me to sit at my computer for seven or eight hours per day. There was little-to-no interaction with my peers, nor was there anything fun to do.

I remember a moment when I was sitting at my computer, completing a test for my career class. The class was about various career fields and how to find which one was right for me. One of the questions on the multiple-choice test was something like, "What kinds of goals should you set for yourself? A) Large and unmanageable B) Small and manageable."

This broke my brain.

I grew up surrounded by people who dreamed BIG no matter what; and even if it took a while to reach their goals, they made it happen. So imagine me, sitting at my desk, staring at the question on my computer screen. Of course I would pick "Large" goals. I love striving for the highest, biggest, and best ideal that I can, even if it's out of my reach *right now.*

I was furious. *How about "large **and** manageable"? Where's that option?! I understand the concept that you should set smaller goals for yourself so that you can reach the larger ones, but why can't I have large goals, too? Is it wrong to have large goals?*

"Mom, come look at this." She turned around, and immediately saw that I was pissed.

I showed her the question on my screen. "They're treating me like I'm a monkey!" I explained the situation to her, and I know that she got a kick out of it — probably boosting her "Momma Pride," hearing that my train of thought was following in her footsteps.

But that was the last straw, signaling to us the need for a new solution as soon as possible.

Flash-forward three months, I'm entering my first improv class at my new school. Flash-forward two years, I'm entering my first mock trial competition to testify on the witness stand. In every performance, I'm laughing with friends and lighting up as I take the stage.

But getting there wasn't rainbows and unicorns. I doubted myself... a lot. Maybe not as much as Harry (*Harry Potter and The Sorcerer's Stone*) did when Hagrid told him he was a wizard. Yet, whenever I was about to do an improv show, take on more mock trial roles, or even now as I'm starting my first business, there is always this voice in my head that tells me that I am not ready for it.

The morning of my State Mock Trial competition, one of those voices manifested as an Australian accent that took over my mind on the drive to the courthouse. The accent linked itself with a character I was going to be playing on the witness stand later that day, and I'm pretty sure my mom was a little worried. (You know, even though she was laughing so hard I was worried she'd pee herself on the way to the courthouse.) It was a great way to cope with the lingering stress of the long day ahead, and it got that doubting voice out of my mind.

And let me tell you, that doubting voice is wrong just about every time. I have some amazing mentors and friends to thank for that. They empowered and equipped me with what I needed to perform well and have an amazing time doing it.

Today, I know myself more deeply—my strengths and my weaknesses—because I took those risks to dive into the uncertain territory of improv and mock trial and now business, and I discovered more of what I'm really made of. I can't imagine life without speaking, without playing, without performing. I'm filled with nervous excitement every time I'm asked to speak but then my inner extrovert comes out in a big way. It lifts me up, pushes me to process things I haven't yet articulated, and constantly teaches me that I'm capable of more than I think I am.

As you read in the introduction, by the time Aaron arrived, I had realized that an individual's body, mind, spirit, and journey are sacred; and my role in everyone's life is to focus on the divinity within them and witness their journey, not shape or carve it out for them. At the core of this belief was another: *People come to this world with purpose and potential and so much of what they need to fulfill it. Our job is to look for it, nurture it, and reflect it back to them until they own it for themselves.*

In other words, a huge part of our journey here and helping others on theirs is deepening self-knowledge. Who are we? What are we here to do? What are our natural superpowers that need to be honed? What do we fear? Where are our limits?

Aaron's childhood was full of moments of him doing something adeptly with hardly any training or coaching at all, and me thinking, *Hmmmm... I wonder.* But you'd find me dead before you'd catch me saying any of that to him. In fact, when people said, "Oh look, you're so good at _____. Maybe you'll be a _____," I bristled and added, "Or anything else you want to be or do in this world."

I wanted *him* to develop the self-knowledge that would guide him through life as he chose which schools he wanted to attend, careers to pursue, and hobbies to enjoy. So, I paid attention, asked questions, and offered invitations to see if they would lead him to unleashing more potential. Hence the story of his love of performing and the maybe-too-many invitations I gave him to cultivate this superpower. (Teehee.)

There was one moment in particular when we brushed up against this topic and I really had to be cautious.

"Mom, it's so sad," he started.

I glanced over at my ten-year-old sitting in the passenger seat. "What's sad?"

"Robson turned eleven, and he didn't get his letter from Hogwarts!" he exclaimed, shaking his head at the misfortune.

Uh oh... I thought. *Does he think Hogwarts is a real place? How have I missed this? How am I going to break this to him?*

"Oh dear, Aaron. That is a bummer..." I stalled, still trying to find my way forward.

"I know, Mom. It's so sad. He's upset and I can understand why."

Knowing that his feelings were more important than the accuracy of his beliefs, especially at the tender age of ten, I decided to play along. The conversation was so unusual that

I decided to dig in and find out where this was coming from. Was my kid living in fantasy land, or was his soul using Story to try to tell me something?

"Aaron, what would you do if you got a letter from Hogwarts? Would you leave Robson behind?"

"Mom, I'd leave *YOU* for Hogwarts!" he exclaimed.

"Wow! You'd leave me?!?! You must really want to go to a magic school, huh?"

"Duh!"

"Well, okay then. Here's hoping you get your letter on your birthday or we somehow find a magical teacher for you."

"Yes, I want it so bad!"

We went home that evening and, of course, watched a *Harry Potter* movie again.

About half-way through it, we paused to get some snacks and I asked, "Aaron, who is your favorite character in this movie?"

"Professor McGonagall!" he said without taking a moment to think about it.

What? Not Harry Potter? Seriously?

"Wow, that's not who I would have guessed. What do you like about her?"

"She is really awesome. She's powerful and kind. She always assumes they are trying to do the right thing, even when they are actually breaking the rules."

"Ah... yes. She is really fair and helpful," I said as I grabbed the bowl of snacks and my drink and headed back to the living room.

As I settled into the couch and waited for Aaron to get himself comfortable, I marveled at our conversations that day and their implications: *I've always known this kid has some serious magic and potential in him, and it sounds like he's aware of it, too. He's ready for the invitation and the teacher to show up. Well, now I know how to pray specifically.*

Diving Deeper into Self-Knowledge with Your Kids and Their Stories

Superpowers

Yes, you and your child both have them. No, not the "magic" or supernatural kind of superpowers, although sometimes that is the case. We're talking about things that you are innately brilliant at doing — the qualities and activities that come naturally to you.

Like most parents, you probably watch your child do things naturally and wonder to yourself if that will turn into a profession or hobby later in their lives, but do you ever get a deep sense of what your child is here to be, or do?

What are some of their innate qualities?
In what activities do they lose themselves for hours?

Which tools do they love to use?

What do they do so quickly and easily
that it makes your head spin?

Do you think they have any awareness of these superpowers, or are they more like Aang (Avatar: The Last Airbender), just going about their business and doing incredible things under the watchful eye of adults who are looking for the next avatar to save the world? Do they understand what the toys or tools they are drawn to say about them and their purpose, like Aang's favorite toys indicated to the monks that he was the hero they'd been waiting for; or do they need to be asked questions that spark their curiosity?

What invitations could you offer to them to nurture
their natural gifts, talents, and obsessions?

Who could you connect them with who shares a similar passion or ability that could help them hone their craft?

Lewis (*Meet The Robinsons*) was eager to create and share his inventions, and in order to fulfill his purpose, he absolutely needed the parents who adopted him and gave him his very own laboratory.

"Kryptonite" (Limits)

Similar to how it weakened Superman, kryptonite is the stuff that steals our strength and sometimes our sanity. However, instead of thinking of it in terms of an external object that cuts us off from our superpowers, we view this as more of internal saboteurs. These are the beliefs and fears that limit and sabotage our best efforts to fulfill our purpose. And, if you think about some of your favorite heroes, you might notice that their kryptonite (the hero's great weakness or limitation) is often deeply connected to their superpower. How many orphaned boys do we have to see develop supernatural powers to protect themselves and fulfill their destiny, only to be almost defeated by the residue of the wounds — the anger and bitterness toward their antagonist, or the fears of not being loved or being abandoned again — at that pivotal moment in their story? Think Anakin (*Star Wars*), using his extraordinary connection to the Force to avenge his mother and destroy the future of the jedis and eventually the known universe.

What does this mean for your children? Well, if you find yourself with a young padawan master-storyteller on your hands, you may notice that a potential "kryptonite" of that superpower is deception. In order to avoid squashing the superpower, we have to find ways to help them own the mastery and then recognize the consequences of mis-using or abusing it.

Which of your child's quirks or "misbehaviors"
are actually just an imbalance of their superpower?

What would happen if you pointed this out to them —
that they were exceptional at _____,
but it isn't good for them or others to use it
in the following ways for the following reasons?

Using Story to Embrace It All

It's so awesome to live in "that zone" or "flow," where we have easy access to our superpowers and can use them to make the world a better place, that we can easily be tempted to keep all of our attention there and ignore the parts of us that are underdeveloped and in need of love and healing. The gift of Story is that it allows us to discuss this dynamic with our children and help them discover their superpowers and their potential kryptonite, and even explore ways to maintain a healthy balance and keep all of them in view and moving toward wholeness, before they are tempted.

One of our favorite things to do is talk about our favorite characters and even notice how those change when we re-engage a story after some time. We just watched a series that had a character that surprised us at every turn with her fierce nature and don't-give-a-shit-what-anyone-thinks actions. We both agreed that we loved her but weren't sure we should and eventually realized that maybe the reason we loved her so much is because it was so easy for her to create and hold boundaries, which is something we were both working on in our relationships and businesses.

What if we can explore the characters and their levels of self-awareness out there, and then use that to deepen our own and our children's in here? Better to walk a mile in their shoes than walk too many into those dark places on our own.

Which characters do your children love?

*What superpowers might they be
seeing reflected back at them?*

*Which kryptonite might they be able to engage before
they have to experience it in their own lives?*

*What can you do to help them deepen their self-knowledge
and use it to guide all of their future choices?*

*Which stories and characters can you use to show them that
heroes who use and expand their superpowers
and figure out how to manage their kryptonite
are the ones who cultivate the
best character and lead a more free life?*

Helping children discover, hone, and expand their super-powers helps them build their confidence and develops a strong foundation for their character. And the awareness of their kryptonite and how to manage it will empower them to keep leaning into their strengths and steer clear of unnecessary suffering.

Chapter Three
Training

"If you leave now, you won't be able to go into the Avatar state at all."

~ Guru Pathik ~

We all sat in the oversized living room with the big screen tv, eager to see Aang begin his training to master the Avatar state. It was something he would have to do if he was going to defeat the Fire Lord and save the world.

"Aang, in order to master the Avatar State, you must open all the chakras…"

As the guru explained what chakras are, how they become blocked, and what it takes to open them again, my husband and I looked at each other and shook our heads in wonder. We had lots of conversations in between episodes about how this "silly little Nickelodeon cartoon" was delivering some of the most profound spiritual insights to small children.

I marveled again as I listened to the guru teach Aang (and Aaron) about the importance of this type of work and not stopping until it was over: "…Be warned, opening the chakras is an intense experience, and once you begin the process, you cannot stop until all seven are open. Are you ready?"

A few tears slipped down my cheek as Aang released the blocks in his chakras one-by-one and I prayed for a mentor who could help me do the same. *What I wouldn't give to have someone sit with me and walk me through my old pain.*

When he got to the last chakra, Aang told the guru that he couldn't let go of his dearest friend, Katara; and as he was trying to open it, he had a vision that she was in trouble. Immediately, he lost his connection to his Avatar self and decided to go save her instead of completing his training.

"No, Aang! If you leave now, you won't be able to go into the Avatar state at all!" the guru shouted after him as he hurried to his flying bison to go save his friend.

I leapt for the remote control, paused the show, and asked, "Aaron, what's going to happen to Aang if he goes to save Katara instead of finishing his training?"

Aaron was already twisted around on the couch, looking at me with a mix of frustration and curiosity. "What... Mom?"

"What do you think will happen to Aang if he goes to save Katara instead of finishing his training?" I repeated myself.

His forehead scrunched up in confusion. He was obviously frustrated that I had paused the show at such a dramatic moment *and* was asking him a tough question. "I don't know, Mom."

"What happened to Luke when he left his training with Yoda early to save his friends?" I offered a clue from the *Star Wars* epic we had just finished watching the night before.

"Oh yeah... it was bad. He didn't save them."

"Right. Instead, he fell into the trap that Vader had set *and* got his hand cut off," I reminded him before giving him another chance to predict the outcome on screen. "So, what do you think might happen if Aang leaves his training early like Luke did?"

"Maybe he won't save them...? Maybe he'll get hurt...?" he wondered aloud, searching for the answer that would let him off the hook and turn his show back on.

"Well, let's see." I pressed play as he repositioned himself to face the tv.

We all sat riveted as Aang arrived at the scene of the battle and fought alongside his friends. Unfortunately, they were outnumbered and outpowered. And Aang, forcing himself into the Avatar state, was near-mortally wounded by one of the lightning strikes directed at him. As he fell to the ground, we all gasped.

"Mom! Just like Luke!" Aaron had turned around on the couch to show me his wide eyes and stunned expression.

All I could do was nod and say, "Yes, I guess it's important to finish training."

Training

What did you learn about training and mentors from your favorite childhood movies, tv series, and books? Well, let's see. A good witch shows up with some advice and magical shoes and then disappears for most of the journey; and then the carefully-sought-out mentor at the end of the story turns

out to be a bit of a fraud *(Wizard of Oz)*. I don't remember
Elliott *(ET)* or any other characters in my early years having
a mentor, except those who needed physical training like
Daniel *(Karate Kid)* and those crime-fighting amphibians
(Teenage Mutant Ninja Turtles). Ren *(Footloose)* did have his
mom supporting him, and the only other guy who gave him
any advice suggested he simply do what he wanted to do so
cleverly that he couldn't actually get into trouble. Hmmmm.
Oh, and then there was Curly *(City Slickers)*, who was an
absolute expert with seemingly very little ability and/or
desire to do anything other than take care of his duties and
frustrate those who reached out for some human connection
and advice. It wasn't until I was a teenager, watching *Dead
Poets Society,* that I actually witnessed a powerful and
relatable mentoring experience ('cause this girl did not
physically train for anything!).

Professor John Keating inspired me like no other
character ever had, and I now know it's because he modeled
a style of mentoring that I knew I needed and also was
someday going to need to embody. Keating didn't offer
answers to his young students; instead, he asked powerful
questions and insisted that his students connect with *their
own* minds, hearts, and desires to answer them. He assumed
they had the answers or the capacity to find them and were
better off knowing *that* sooner than later. Like Miyagi (*Karate
Kid*) and Splinter (*Teenage Mutant Ninja Turtles*), he deeply
believed in his students and carefully nurtured relationships
beyond the expected delivery of knowledge, never missing
a moment outside of training to connect and support. Very
much like Ren's mother and co-worker, he supported them in

finding their own way and offered just enough of an idea for them to pursue and own it for themselves.

These varying stories of training have definitely impacted my own journey of being a mentee and eventually a mentor. Though I did not participate in much physical training, most of the adult figures in my life who were in positions to train me (parents, teachers, coaches, etc.) did their job with a particular mindset or posture that they likely learned from their own training experiences. The mindset is that of "I'm the one with the knowledge and you're the empty container that needs me to fill you up with the right knowledge and skills." Fortunately, there were a few true mentors who saw my "magic egg" and nurtured it with insightful stories, customized learning opportunities, and basic human kindness and empathy. And, when I got to the university, I was given my very own Professor Keating. He inspired me with his vision of young people owning, embodying, and sharing their own hard-earned spiritual journey through stories and projects that would change the world. He ignored my fear-ridden objections and accepted me into the honors program. And, most telling, he took the time to sit with and learn *from me.*

If I'm honest, this guy kinda ruined me for other mentors for the rest of my life. He set the bar pretty high with these two statements, which pretty much embody everything I loved about my experience with him and seek to provide as a guide to others: "If you walk out of here with more answers than questions, I haven't done my job," and "If you were to really look past the eyes, into the soul of a person, you would be tempted to worship them." And yet, I've been blessed with others who met that expectation and surpassed it. The woman who asked me what value I had to give to the world at twenty-seven years old is one of the smartest people and most amazing educators I know, and she spent a ton of time showing me how to take my teaching to the next level.

About the time we were watching Aang and Guru Pathik work through his blocks to the Avatar state, two lifetime mentors and gurus in their own right entered my life. There was the woman who helped me take the longest journey I've ever taken — the one from my head to my heart. She sat with me in my frustrated tears, she listened and offered other possible perspectives, she called out all of my shit, and she let me move at my own pace (which was excruciatingly slow). More than a mentor, I eventually looked to her as a spiritual mother because she had earned the title with all of that labor. And then there was the angel-like mindset and sales coach who showed up in my life the year I decided to grow a business — a woman who pulled me up simply by modeling the power of intention, clarity, and inspired action. Instead of trying to keep my dreams and expectations "reasonable," she said, "Go for it!" and helped me navigate the obstacles, detours, and potholes I encountered along the way.

I've also experienced my fair share of terrible mentors — people who treated me as more of a project than a person, disempowered me by giving me easy answers, and manipulated and/or betrayed me when their egos were threatened by my emerging mastery.

As I shared in the introduction, I was pretty darn careful about who I invited into Aaron's space when he was very young. I vetted them based on not just their love for him, but their natural response to his superpowers and their approach to training. Those who cringed when he spoke his truth, had big feelings, or asked insightful questions, and those who were locked in an old paradigm of "fill this child up with what he needs to know" spent very little time with him until I was confident about his ability to question and challenge what he was hearing. Fortunately, there were several people in my growing community who smiled, leaned in, and asked powerful questions when they saw him shining brightly or struggling with something. Those were the folks that I invited to hang out with him and the ones I asked to be part of his Life & Love Advisory Council when he turned twelve. They all quickly agreed to be allies and guides in their respective expertise, but none of them seemed to be quite the Professor McGonagall he craved.

My Learning Happens Everywhere

I threw open the back door and stomped through it with my frustrating day at school replaying in my mind.

Why does he do that? It's so annoying. Why don't the teachers do anything? Why won't he stop?

A classmate had been acting up in the classroom, and I couldn't understand why. It seemed to bother everyone else, too; and no matter how much she tried, my teacher could hardly do anything about it.

Twelve-year-old me understood that sometimes people make bad choices, but I didn't understand *why* they make them. I certainly couldn't grasp why some people make the same bad choices over and over again.

I continued down the main hallway and into the dining room where I slung my backpack and thwomped it onto the ground. My mom was working on her laptop at the dining room table and, noticing my irked presence, welcomed me home.

"Hi, buddy. How was your day?" she inquired.

Exhaling the stress of the day, I let out a half-hearted, "Good."

She raised her eyebrows, her mommy senses obviously tingling. "Yeah? You sure?"

I'm not hiding this very well.

Holding back an eye roll, I pursed my lips as I scoured the kitchen for a snack. "There's someone at school who doesn't listen. It makes everyone feel... bad. I wish he would stop."

"Oh, I'm so sorry. Do you wanna talk about it?" She closed her laptop, signaling that she was giving me her full attention.

"I just don't understand why he does it."

She cocked her head and narrowed her eyes in deep thought. "Well, you never know. Maybe he's having trouble at home or something. Sometimes, people's situations can be challenging and affect how they feel and act in public."

I walked in silence for a moment as I carried my snack to the table where she sat before asking, "What do you mean?"

"It's sort of like... *Ponyo*," she started.

Ponyo? The little fish girl who grew unsatisfied with life under the sea with her dad and then rebelled, escaping to the surface where she caused all kinds of mischief? It seemed like an appropriate parallel. *Well, not exactly.*

"I'm still not sure I understand. Ponyo did get into some trouble, but she learned how to control herself."

"Right, but she had a good teacher to show her how to regulate herself; she had Sōsuke."

I wasn't buying it. "But the kid in class, the teacher tries to show him how to... regulate?" She nodded her head, affirming I used the word in the correct context. "But he doesn't seem to change."

"Yeah, sometimes it's harder than it was for Ponyo. Different people have different experiences. It takes time."

I raised my eyebrows and looked down at the table, taking a big bite of my granola bar. "Alright." I was still having trouble understanding and empathizing.

My mom sat back in her chair with her arms crossed. "You know, I think we should go to MTS."

"What's that again?" I asked, puzzled. I knew that she had mentioned it before, but I didn't really know what it was.

"It's a workshop where teens get an opportunity to talk about all the stuff they don't feel comfortable talking about anywhere else. They teach basic communication and life skills..." She paused. "Yeah, you're just about a teen, anyway."

To be honest, I wasn't stoked by the opportunity, but I was open to it if it would help me sort through this situation and others like it.

A few months went by, and there we were in the car on our way to the event. I remember watching as the California palm trees, bikers, and beaches shone through the passenger-side window. I felt like I knew what to expect, but I had no idea how my perspective about the workshop and so much more was about to shift dramatically.

We pulled into the packed conference center parking lot and got out of the car.

Wow, that's a lot of people.

My body quickly became overwhelmed with a constricting social anxiety as I began to notice how much older the vast majority of the other teens were. It was hard to imagine how I'd belong in or relate to a group that was more aged than I.

We made our way inside, grabbed our nametags, caught up with some of my mom's friends that she met when she used to help run the program, and we took our seats.

After the introduction, the workshop facilitators guided us through some exercises that got everyone connected with each other. I had some great adult partners who I was able to talk to about some of the things I was facing in my life. (I later realized they intentionally partnered with me because of how young I was.) We looked into each other's eyes, shared our deepest stories and struggles, and allowed ourselves to be open to finding new ways to navigate the world. This one-on-one sharing process gave me some much-needed perspective into what others had previously and were currently going through. But, what I heard wasn't earth-shattering by any means.

Eventually, it came time to take some of these conversations to the entire room. We re-arranged our chairs to face the front stage as the facilitators fanned out across the room with microphones, handing them to everyone that wanted to speak. The room grew quiet, and I remember listening intently to one kid in particular who wasn't much younger than I was. He shared sensitive and heartbreaking stories involving loss, addiction, and depression that you wouldn't even begin to think a young person could go through. I was confounded. Others stood up, young people you would never think were struggling, and shared stories, secrets, and feelings they had bottled inside for years.

I had no idea.

I was, and still am, extremely blessed to have such a safe, loving life full of opportunity. Compared to what I heard, situations that I considered to be "tough" seemed like such small problems.

After the workshop, everything clicked. I had gained a new understanding of hardship and adversity, and perhaps the greater gift was the opportunity to learn from other's *mistakes*. I now understand that there can be so much more happening behind the scenes than what somebody lets you see. Their situations, hardships, and stories created wildly different experiences than I would ever have expected.

I also realized that this was the reason my mom brought me to the workshop and, in a broader sense, intentionally shared her own stories and challenges (in an age-appropriate way, of course). She wanted me to learn from her mistakes and be more prepared than she was for those challenges in my own life. I can't tell you how much this approach has helped me detect and avoid harmful situations.

It reminded me of the last few episodes of *Avatar: The Last Airbender* where Aang was about to face his greatest challenge yet, but he wasn't sure how to do it in a way that was in alignment with his values. He called on the previous Avatars to offer him advice based on their experiences—both triumphs and failures—and from that wisdom, he was able to forge his own path.

In addition to learning from others' mistakes, I was finding things out on my own. From preschool up until second grade, I attended a Montessori school where I was mostly responsible for my own learning. I had hands-on experience with different materials and tools that allowed me to learn the basics of math and reading and then hone my skills and follow my curiosity.

After Montessori, I went to a charter school where I was partly homeschooled and became responsible for getting my work done by myself. That opportunity introduced me to the internet and, with it, a seemingly infinite pool of learning possibilities. I became involved with online communities and learned project management strategies, put into practice some problem-solving mindsets, and obtained many valuable lessons from a lot—and I mean *a lot*—of mistakes, headaches, and heartbreaks.

I felt like Lewis (*Meet The Robinsons*), following my passion and learning how to figure things out on my own, especially when something blew up in my face. And other times, I felt like Nemo (*Finding Nemo*), taking a quick day trip to explore with a friend or on a grand adventure to Australia, gaining insights into the worlds outside my own.

Over the years, I've also had some great opportunities to learn from all kinds of great Uncle Iroh-like (*Avatar: The Last Airbender*) mentors. When I was younger, that meant getting destroyed at chess by Aunt Kate or being pushed to figure out how to build a computer on my own with the help of a family friend. Their riddles, metaphors, and hands-off approaches may have pissed me off a good bit, but it was well worth it. Kind of like how Korra (*The Legend of Korra*) experienced training with her mentors, complaining and moaning because she didn't get it right the first time or they refused to just give her the damn answers.

I had some more structured learning, too, with piano and violin, but I ended up walking away early before my training was complete. Now, I don't think I'll end up losing a limb like Luke (*Star Wars*) because of it, but I wish I had stayed with piano in particular.

And more recently, I've had some of the most influential mentoring experiences I've ever had—from knowledgeable teachers who love what they do, family friends that are showing me the ropes, and new friends that have allowed me to observe them while they kick butt and take names.

No matter my path or ambition, the most meaningful training comes from seeing new perspectives and understanding that learning from mistakes and failures is just as important as learning from skill and successes.

You better believe I was on the lookout for who would be his Professor McGonagall, and I did invite him to hang out with several folks who I thought might be The One. Funny thing was, it was *his* self-knowledge that led him to the place and the people who would help him nurture his potential. That moment he realized that he needed a better environment in which to learn was a turning point for him. I'd known that online learning wasn't a fit for a while, but I knew he had to see it for himself before he would be willing to try something else. When he finally saw it and said, "I'm ready," he soon found himself in a self-directed learning community with two teachers that would help him reconnect with his love of performing and learning. And one of them — you can't make this shit up — was known on campus for her love of everything Hogwarts. Aaron's self-knowledge had led him straight to his very own Professor McGonagall, who saw his potential and called it forth.

Over the last few years, I have watched Aaron vet his mentors very carefully. Like my Professor Keating, his Professor McGonagall set the bar pretty high. Powerful questions. Lots of belief in him. Incredible opportunities to try and fail and get up and really truly learn. Appropriate amounts of acknowledgment, celebration, and inviting him to his own next level. The mentors he has chosen since, for everything from developing more self-knowledge to growing his business and expanding his skillset, all play in the exact same way. And when they don't, well... he usually shifts the relationship or moves on. This momma couldn't ask for more than that.

Diving Deeper into Training
with Your Kids and Their Stories

Training Required

Without people who have "been there and done that" to guide us, we would be left to create something from nothing with absolutely no model with which to begin. Story and life experience have proven that some mentors and approaches are better than others.

At its core, the conversation about Mentoring really revolves around *learning*. What is important to know? How do we actually come to know something? What is required to know it? Who can teach us? If you look at the beliefs and/or default assumptions around learning in our culture, you will see that we are operating as though we believe:

- **Answers are More Important than Questions:** Parents, teachers, and other authorities tend to deliver information rather than cultivate a learning opportunity/experience with powerful questions.

- **Learning is A Mental Activity:** Information, answers, data, processes, etc. engage the mind primarily and do not create space for the other parts of the learner — the body, the soul, or the spirit.

- **Children are Empty Vessels that Need Filling:** Delivering information and insisting on memorization, regurgitation, and compliance creates a one-way track for learning.

- **Teachers/Mentors and Learners are Not Equals:** The one-way track for learning creates and maintains a sense that the Parent/Teacher/Mentor is the only one with the answers.

- **Everything We Need to Know is External:** The "empty vessel" and "inequality with elders" leaves the learner with a sole reliance on external resources for information and learning.

- **Outcomes are More Important than The Process:** Grades, tests, and checklists are the established ways to measure what we have learned.

- **Learning Happens in Classrooms:** There are very specific spaces where learning takes place.

We could go on and on about these assumptions, but the point we are making here is that the current paradigm for learning treats us more like machines than people. Data in; data out. Questions would indicate that we think the learner might have something of value to add to the learning process, that they might even have something to offer the Mentor/Teacher, that some knowledge is innate and intuitive, and that the process of learning requires a meaningful goal and a relationship where both parties feel safe, respected, and capable of navigating a process together.

Of course, this makes our current situation make a lot of sense, doesn't it? Machines work until they don't. Hello, workaholism. Machines don't feel or relate. Hello, higher rates of depression and anxiety, substance abuse, and suicide. Machines don't vet the information input. Hello, loss of agency and freedom.

In this culture, we move from parents (doing the best they can) who are so busy that it's easier to just give an answer than to ask a question into classrooms with teachers who are professionally obligated to make sure learners can regurgitate information and pass tests. Professors and bosses then provide us with the answers required to achieve goals for survival. And then eventually, when we get tired of feeling like machines, we hire therapists and coaches. The problem is that the paradigm has been firmly set in place. Therapists and coaches are asked to provide answers, and sometimes they do because, hey — they were raised in the same paradigm!

Those are not the mentors we're looking for — for ourselves or our children.

A New Paradigm for Training

More You
You are your child's first mentor and model. How you activate, cultivate, and engage their learning process will set the tone for every future learning and mentor experience. And you never stop being their first and always mentor.

More Meaning
We all know what it's like to be forced to learn something we don't want to learn and don't see any use for. Sure, our teachers told us that we would need that information or skill someday, but did we really? Wouldn't it have been so much more fun and fruitful if we had been invited to learn something that meant something to us?

What does your child really want to know? What are their interests? How could you create opportunities for them to pursue that knowledge/experience?

What natural talents and skills are emerging in your child? Which characters are increasing (or could increase) their enthusiasm for cultivating those talents and skills?

In what situations or environments would those be nurtured and cultivated with curiosity?

Which fictional mentors are your children already drawn to and how could you use this knowledge to find a real-life guide that they would love?

When we ask children to pursue what is meaningful to them, they are less likely to disengage from learning and growth and more likely to continue to pursue their passions throughout adulthood. Lewis (*Meet the Robinsons*) was fortunate enough to find parents who were also passionate about inventions and had the knowledge and resources required to nurture the genius that was clearly trying to emerge in this young boy. In contrast, when Troy (*High School*) discovered that he loved acting as much as basketball, his father wasn't too thrilled about another activity competing for his son's attention. Of course, once he saw Troy on stage, he realized his son's natural talent and supported his pursuit of its cultivation.

More Questions Than Answers

It's not easy to stop the Answer Train, especially because most of us are so damn busy. It takes less time and effort to spit out our answer than it does to pause, make eye contact, and get curious in a conversation. And yet, let's be honest, it's those moments when we feel the most connected to ourselves, each other, and the world around us. Curiosity connects.

*What are the most common answers
you hear yourself offering?*

*What question could you ask to invite your child to
participate in a learning experience with you instead?*

*Which characters in their favorite books or movies
like to ask questions? When could you take the
opportunity to point out what great questions the
character is asking, and maybe how the questions
are part of what helps them on their journey?*

*What questions could you ask your child
to propel their learning forward?*

What questions does your child have?
How can you help your child fall in love with questions?

These questions, and the simple experience of being asked these questions, creates a pattern of inquiry for children. They will begin internalizing the questions and asking them and delivering answers before we can answer them. This one skill we develop within them will be a huge part of how they develop their character and preserve their freedom throughout their lives. It was not a parent-child relationship, but over the course of their relationship, Ron began to ask the right questions and get to answers before Hermione did (*Harry Potter*) because curiosity and learning were superpowers she had modeled from the beginning. In one of our favorite episodes, *Lucifer* transmutes his panic into problem-solving with the question, "What would the detective do?" Suddenly, he realizes being around her has unconsciously taught him how to solve crimes. Just like Hermione, you might be surprised and get a little, "Always a tone of surprise" response to your astonished look or tone.

More Body, Soul, and Spirit
How much of the information, answers, data, processes, etc. you learned in school do you actually remember? Facts, dates, and other details mean nothing and fail to stick with us because we are not *just* mental beings. But what happens when we add the body, the soul, and the spirit to the equation? What happens when the history teacher replaces dry PowerPoints full of dates and facts with costumes, simulations of moments in history, and questions about how people during that time may have felt?

One of our absolute favorite scenes of all time is that of Professor Keating (*Dead Poets Society*) giving his students an embodied experience of the concept of and natural tendency toward conformity. Instead of a dry lecture, he took them into the courtyard and asked them to begin walking around the space in their own style. Immediately, they began to walk at their own stride and pace, with a unique posture and cadence. But after just a few moments, they all fall into step with each other. They weren't trying; it just happened. When he brings their attention to what just took place without their conscious awareness, he reflects back to them this bigger concept of conformity and the difficulty of maintaining one's own beliefs in the face of others' but the beauty and power of finding "their own walk" through the world. Whew! That's some powerful teaching!

Learners remember every detail of the *experience* because it required their whole body to engage the learning process. What happens when we replace dry statements of potential consequences with well-written books or movies and say, "Why do you think that terrible thing happened to that character?" Learners put themselves in the shoes of the character and learn through the activation of their body, soul, and spirit, just as much as their mind.

> *Which books or movies would help your child*
> *get a more holistic learning experience around a*
> *theme that is important to them right now?*

> *Which characters do they admire, and how*
> *could you use their holistic experience of that*
> *character to create a learning experience?*

> *How can you create moments and experiences that activate*
> *their body, soul, and spirit to fully engage in the learning?*

Even when they find themselves in environments that focus on their minds, we will have built a pattern and co-developed some strategies for them to immerse their whole selves into their learning.

More Innate Knowledge and Intuition Than Information
Have you ever wondered how sometimes, you just know
something? You can't really articulate *how* you know it,
but you do. Some people just know stuff. They're naturally
good with words or numbers or music or people. Have you
ever noticed how sometimes that information resonates
with information you're receiving from external sources,
and sometimes it really doesn't? You may not hear audible
whispers or be inspired to sing "Into the Unknown" like Elsa
(*Frozen II*), but you intuitively know what is true and what
isn't, or what you should or shouldn't do; and you can't
always explain why or how, but eventually you find out you
were right. Your innate knowledge and intuition may have
been dismissed, shamed, or neglected, but that doesn't
mean it isn't there and you can't trust it.

What does your child appear to know innately?
How does your child's intuition show up regularly?

What if you raised your child to value what they know
intuitively just as much (or maybe even more) than
what they are learning from outside sources?

What if you asked them what they think or feel about
information they're receiving or questions they are asking?

Which characters in their favorite movies and books
demonstrate the power of intuition and innate knowledge?

When will you take the opportunity to point that
fact out and applaud it in front of your child?

If we give children the gift of owning their innate knowledge
and intuition, they will be less likely to blindly follow or
comply with what doesn't feel good or true for them. This
truly is one of the most important pathways to preserving
personal and collective freedom.

More Relationship Than Data

We can't learn if we don't feel safe, loved, and respected. As soon as one of those is breached, flight, fight, or freeze kicks in and shuts down our access to the parts of our brain required for learning, making connections, and storing information. What creates that sense of safety for us? The people with whom we are trying to learn and whether they treat us with love and respect.

In what ways do you (or could you) see your child as your equal — in life and the learning process? What might you be able to learn from (or remember through) them?

How can you make relationship just as important as the information or skill being learned?

What stories can you tell to let your child know that you have experienced similar adventures or challenges?

Which of their favorite stories can you use to point out the importance of mentors and guides who really care — and how they demonstrate that care in the relationship?

What if you asked your child how they would like you to support their adventure? Give them some options: Observer/Cheerleader, Ally/Collaborator, etc.

Unless and until our school systems are reformed, *we* are the ones responsible for modeling and cultivating healthy relationships. Just by being in relationships with them intentionally, we can give them the experience of (and set the standard for) healthy boundaries, good communication, and maintaining a sense of self and agency when in relationship with others. Uncle Iroh (*Avatar: The Last Airbender*) rarely told his nephew what to do; instead, he invited him to sit with him over tea and simply modeled a more balanced approach to life and defending what was right and good. It was his love for Zuko that kept the young man from completely destroying himself and held open the possibility for him to choose to be the hero instead of the villain he had been cast as in his family, his nation, and the overall narrative.

More Process Than Outcome

We spend so much more time in the process of learning than in the moment of AHA. The time spent in studying is greater than the time spent taking the test or receiving the grade. Yet we can become so focused on those momentary outcomes that we miss out on the juicy experiences available in the process. Worse yet, we discount some of the elements of the process itself — questions, challenges, problem-solving, faith- or resilience-building, etc. — when that's where most of the personal growth, character-building, and learning takes place. Of course, when we have children who are neurodiverse and learn differently, this focus on outcome over process is one of the reasons for traumatic learning experiences.

What is your child's approach to learning? What does their process look like? Do they approach it in an orderly fashion or do they dive into the chaos and emerge with some order?

Which characters in their favorite stories have a similar process that you could point out and applaud the next time you engage them together?

How can you make "their process" visible to them — help them see and understand how they learn most effectively? (How did you do this? Where did you start? Why did you decide to go in this direction?)

Just be careful and make sure that you're doing this from a place of curiosity, and without any judgment about their process or outcome. In other words, remember to keep Safety and Curiosity at the center of all of your questions.

Think about Ray (*Field of Dreams*) and how it's the faith he builds along the journey of acting on the whispers to "build it and they will come," the friendships he develops along the way, and the moments of understanding *why* he was inspired that make the outcome so powerful for himself and the audience. We might even argue that who the characters of *Lord of The Rings* become (the true king, the courageous hobbits, the friendly dwarf) is just as important as the fact that they worked together to save Middle Earth.

We feel like there might be an important warning or disclaimer here: It's really important to model this principle. In other words, it's not as useful to point out a child's process and help them celebrate the details of it if we, ourselves, are operating on this "outcome paradigm." One of our tricks has been "inviting each other into our learning processes" rather than just letting the other see the cool "endings" (good grades, bestselling books, big events, etc.). While we are in the process of learning and creating, we ask each other what the other thinks, sees, what questions they might ask, what decisions they would be making, etc. We work through it all and learn together, often coming up with better solutions than we would have on our own.

More Learning Opportunities
You remember that old saying, "When the student is ready, the teacher appears"? Well, we have found that to be true, but not in the way that you might expect. The truth is that we have never sought out mentors and maybe it's because we spent so much time in Story that we witnessed the right person always showing up for the hero. Right when these heroes had reached the limits of their superpowers, mentors like Guru Pathik (*Avatar: The Last Airbender*), Obi-Wan Kenobi (*Star Wars*), and Morpheus (*The Matrix*) would show up in their world. We've never thought, "I need to learn this," and then done a bunch of research to find the right person to help us. And yet, we've always had a

mentor — coaches, friends, colleagues, and even clients who were *obviously* written into our stories at exactly the right time... sometimes before we even knew we needed them.

Because of this, we've developed a mindset that we hope you will consider and maybe even cultivate in your child — that when we are ready, help is already here or on its way.

How would it change your behavior if it were true that mentors appeared when students were ready?

In which of your child's favorite stories do you see evidence of this, and when will you point this out the next time you're experiencing them together?

What if your Co-Author (The Universe, God, Your Higher Self, The Force — whatever you call it) is way ahead of you — already placing the right mentors and answers in your path?

And what if these mentors are the little ones you are raising, the sweet old ladies in line at the grocery store, or the character who inspires you the most in that show you're obsessed with right now?

Training: Don't Do Life Without It

With a proper mentor, we realize that it's more tedious and often painful to dig inside ourselves for answers and courage than it would be to just receive and regurgitate answers. But it's also far less meaningful. We recognize that we would give up if not for the brave few who refuse the temptations to elevate themselves and instead jump into the foxholes with us, and commit to paying forward the presence and patience they received during their training. We learn the consequences of stopping short of completion and persevere through challenges, even when we have the best reasons to pause or stop altogether. ("But LOVE though!") And, we are invited to consider the possibility that learning is an inside-out experience, which opens us up to the opportunity to be mentored by anyone at any time.

Chapter Four
Camaraderie

"You're the one who is weak.
You will never know love or friendship.
And I feel sorry for you."

~ Harry Potter ~

Even though we had watched the series half a dozen times already, I still felt a tear slip down my cheek and glanced at Aaron to see his reaction to this incredible moment when Harry declares that it's his friends, not his magic, that make him more powerful than the villain determined to take his life.

No tears? Hmmm. Makes sense, I guess. He hasn't exactly experienced the type of camaraderie that Harry has with Hermione and Ron. But I have... I know the treasure of friends who will go into the dark unknown with you and stick by you no matter what demons emerge.

I turned my attention from Aaron back to the large television that towered above us. Sprawled out on the foam mattress we always rolled out for an epic series event, both of us were on our backs, heads raised by pillows. And of course, the dogs were sleeping between us.

I've watched this scene so many times, and it hasn't stood out to me like this before. It must be because I literally feel like Harry right now. On the ground, suffering after a fight with a villain in my life, but surrounded by people who love me and have my back. I pray that he has friends like this someday — camarades who will use all of their superpowers to support him, who share a common vision, and who will pick him up when he falls.

Faces of friends and memories of them helping me through my darkest times floated across my mind as we watched the remainder of the movie. There was my oldest friend, who walked beside me while my religious identity shattered and reformed. There were the few "fox hole buddies" who helped me dig through the pain in my past to find the treasure in my story.

And now I have this beautiful group of friends, fellow messengers who want to change the world, circling up in my business and working together to heal our stories and share our messages. They have literally been holding me through this experience of betrayal, helping me to sort through what's mine and what's not and take appropriate steps to heal and bring whatever resolution is possible.

"Aaron, can you think of a hero that saves the world by themself?" I asked as I turned the tv off, set the remote down, and sat up so that I could look at him.

His eyebrows furrowed in thoughtfulness for a few moments. "No, I can't think of one. They all have friends who help them out. Avatar had Katara and Sokka. Luke had Han and Leia. Troy had Chad."

"Yeah, we need good friends because we all go through hard times and face our own villains. That's why I always call your Aunt Kate my 'Sam Wise.'"

"What?" He cocked his head curiously.

"Well, when I went to college and started to question my beliefs, I lost many of my relationships and felt a lot like Frodo from *The Lord of the Rings.* I was on a quest for truth and felt scared and alone. Your Aunt Kate was one of the few people who stayed by my side, even though she was struggling with the big questions, too. You know that scene where Frodo sneaks away to travel to Mordor himself and Sam finds him floating away in a canoe?"

Aaron smiled. "Oh yeah, and he jumps in the water to follow him even though he can't swim?"

"Yep. That was your Aunt Kate. She jumped into water she could barely swim in herself to make sure that I didn't go alone. And we've been 'saving each other' through our different life challenges ever since. It hasn't always been easy. We have disagreed, fought, and even taken time apart like Ron did when he was upset at Harry and Hermione. But we always find our way back to each other. That's the type of friend I know you'll find someday."

He nodded and smiled.

Camaraderie

What did you learn about friendship from your favorite childhood movies, tv series, and books? Did your favorite characters have no friends, a few really close friends, or lots of superficial ones? Were they introverts who had to learn how to be and work with people in order to achieve a goal, or risk-takers who had to slow down to help others? Did they struggle along their path alone or did they lean on their allies while facing challenges? Was there pressure for them to fit a mold, or were their differences in opinions and superpowers respected and even appreciated? Did they make sacrifices for each other and struggle together? Were there relationships full of conflict and drama, or did friends work through their upsets and betrayals in healthy ways?

When I look at my list, I see a few interesting patterns. First, a lot of the tv shows I watched were family-focused, meaning that family members were friends with each other but there weren't a lot of external relationships. Of course, there was Elliott (*E.T.*) who made friends with an alien and then had to let go of him. Ren McCormick (*Footloose*) found himself in a small town where he was not understood but lucky to find one not-so-clever-but-ever-so-sweet companion and a young woman who was looking for someone to help her escape small-town thinking. In fact, many of the movies I loved (*My Girl* and *Benny and Joon*) had characters who just didn't fit in but found another outcast to be their friend and love them despite, and sometimes, for their quirks. Finally, I can't leave out the soap operas I used to watch with my aunt, where betrayal was the norm and usually compounded instead of resolved; and of course, *90210* helped to bring that to the teen experience, too.

Now that you have identified some of the patterns, take a minute and think about your own experience of friendship. Was it easy for you to make friends, or have good relationships always seemed to elude you or be so challenging that you've decided to just go it alone? Are you one of those who just never seemed to fit in, or were you the one who camouflaged easily and then ended up feeling inauthentic, unseen, and maybe even resentful? In friendships, are you the one to make all the sacrifices? Do you struggle with communicating your feelings and asking for what you need, or maybe holding others accountable when they have failed to live up to their word?

Most of my favorite characters struggled to fit in and find good friends, and many of the stories I watched primed me to believe that friendship was hard, full of sacrifice, betrayal, and big drama. Without the opportunity to challenge the narratives or at least get some perspective, these stories became my stories: Loner who didn't fit in, struggled desperately to find and keep friends until high school, and lost all but a few good friendships to serious drama and betrayals until I began to work through these patterns from my adulthood. While Aaron and I were neck-deep in the magical world of *Harry Potter* the first time around, I was immersed in my own school of transformation and not quite managing a lot of mischief with my new allies. It had been ten years since I'd dared to connect with another human being this transparently, allowing them to see all the kryptonite as I worked to hone my superpowers; and it was the beginning of a whole new chapter of camaraderie.

Aaron and I have had lots of big conversations about friendship because they are not only an important part of the stories we have watched together, but they haven't come easy for either of us outside of our living room.

Finally! My People!

"I guess I'm out, then." The words left my mouth in disappointment (and relief) and entered the headphones of some of the friends I had met online. I had worked with them on a video game passion project for almost two years when I finally decided to leave.

The project was really struggling. We had been working for so long with the hope of making meaningful income, but to no avail. I put so much time and effort into the project, and it had come such a long way. The concept was great, but the execution was flawed. People drama, money drama. Broken promises, broken trust.

The first problem was our culture. New team members came around quite frequently, offering to volunteer their time and expertise. But a lot of the time, they didn't last very long because the larger sense of connection and friendship—in my opinion—seemed to be reserved mostly for the "higher-ups" while the newbies were left mostly disconnected.

I think that a lot of it had to do with our desperate need for more help. We recruited just about anyone competent enough to learn how to do a job and were willing to volunteer their time. We were evaluating people for nothing more than what they were good at as opposed to taking into account how they would work within our team as colleagues and as friends. We asked more questions like, "Can you do this ___?" and "How much time can you dedicate to the job?" rather than the questions that older companies tend to ask regarding culture (because they understand how important a healthy one is) like, "How do you work with teams?" and "Would you be open to participating in fun staff events?"

When they arrived, they were usually excited and wanting to integrate with the team and the culture. But the culture, at least among us higher-ups, wasn't very open. We were *accepting* their friendship rather than choosing it because we wanted their skills more than we wanted to *know* them, and that created a rift.

I say "we" throughout because I was guilty of this myself. For a few months, I was responsible for recruitment and onboarding of new team members. I saw first hand how many new recruits were brought in to monitor our broader community but were never really invited to be a part of the internal team. They were left to do the work without the connection from the project managers and had to find connection among themselves. And when you're volunteering your time, belief in the project and connection to others who believe in it is everything.

Yet, I never did much about any of it.

This led to a lot of "lower-ranking" members becoming demotivated, and eventually, they'd go MIA. We never really let them know how much they meant to the team — how much we appreciated their work, regardless of whether it was easy or hard, time consuming or not.

I'm not saying that we ignored them completely — it was quite the opposite. But a lot of things that we did (or *failed* to do) as management kept them separated from us in more than just a professional way like you'd expect from a group of managers versus the employees they managed.

People were leaving because of a sense of not belonging or even betrayal. The amount of work that everyone put in without much in return was taking its toll. Most of us understood that and were working through it, but the straw that broke the camel's back was when we discovered the founder of the project wasn't being transparent about what was happening with the profits we were all involved in creating. Most of the higher-ups were promised returns in the future when/if the money started to come in, so we felt as though we should know where the profits were going. Were they being reinvested? Saved up? Drained from upkeep expenses? Eventually, we found out they were going toward the founder's personal budget almost entirely. And honestly, who could blame him? Times were hard. He had just moved to an upper-class spot in California and had (to our knowledge) no other sources of income.

But if the project wasn't growing, and the money we were making wasn't being reinvested for advertising or upgrades, the writing on the wall became clear to most of the management team.

It was an accidental betrayal. A breaking of trust. The lack of transparency from the beginning around where the money was going, although understandable, left us feeling hopeless and misled.

This was a repeating pattern in my early teens. I craved to be a part of a bigger project, team, and goal and, most importantly, to do something that I love—write stories. And then the betrayal would happen. I've lost time, money, and good friends. It's no wonder I had issues making friends for a while after all of that... always on the lookout for the next inevitable betrayal.

That's why it was impossible for me to stay with the project at that point. The scars from past betrayals demanded that I walk away like Koda (*Brother Bear*) did when he learned that Kenai had killed his mother. While I knew that it wasn't an intentional betrayal, how could I trust the head of the project anymore?

I felt like Goob (*Meet The Robinsons*) after Lewis kept him up so late at night that he missed the winning catch at his baseball game. After that moment, his animosity toward Lewis (and life itself) grew and his future took a turn for the worse. While it isn't an exact comparison to my situation, my trust was broken and resentment started to seep through; and I've seen enough betrayals to know where that leads.

The one thing that was always missing—the one thing I never *really* knew how to go out of my way to create—was genuine connection. And hey, it's a lot harder to do over the internet than it is in person.

About three years later, I met who I consider to be my best friends (Yes, Julian. You, too.)—a bunch of nerds who practice mock trial and play video games, both of which we did together quite frequently.

I love these guys a whole lot. So much, in fact, that we just constantly tease each other. Don't worry, it's definitely reciprocal... I make sure of it.

Looking back, I think our level of comfort and trust is a result of what we've been through together. And no, I'm not talking about the video games; I'm talking about mock trial.

In short, mock trial is a program where you and your team prepare both sides (plaintiff/prosecution and defense) of a fake legal case and compete against other mock trial teams. While that may seem like just a "fun extracurricular," we didn't treat it like that. For many of us, it was all-consuming.

Preparing for and *doing* mock trial is a *lot* of work. We met at least twice a week for practices; and as we got closer to the day(s) of competition, we'd meet just about every day for several hours at a time. And performing at the competitions is a whole other fiasco. Some competitions required us to compete in as many as five rounds, with each of those lasting about three hours. Of course, in the interest of transparency, I can't say that *all* of that time we spent together was one-hundred percent productive, buuut... I think you probably get what I'm going for here.

My *point* here is that we did this really time-consuming and challenging thing together—several times, in fact—racking up nine 2nd place spots in a row during my two years on the team. My hunger for being a part of a bigger project, team, and goal was satisfied; *and* I was doing something I loved... acting. Yes, Mom, I admit it.

Plus, everyone became known for their unique skills and contributions to the team, whether that be the badass expert witness, the lawyer who destroyed other teams' closing arguments nine times out of ten, the witness that could make a "boring" character in the case come alive, the opening statement deliverers that always shared especially compelling stories of the case, or the master of pre-trial arguments that did the thing that literally nobody else on the team wanted to do so incredibly well. Everyone had something special they brought, and we made sure that we played to those strengths.

Fair warning: What I'm about to say is very cheesy, but it's true. The practice, the procrastination, and *especially* the pressure brought us closer together. Our friendships were forged in (figurative) fire. Sure, it wasn't *quite* like Frodo and Sam's almost-literal journey into fire at Mt. Doom (*The Lord of the Rings*), but the same principle still applies. Frodo's bond with Sam, Gandalf, and the rest of the fellowship became unbreakable by the end of their tumultuous quest.

Maybe a better comparison is when Korra (*The Legend of Korra*) joined the Fire Ferrets and competed alongside Bolin and Mako in Republic City's pro-bending tournament. And that was just the beginning of a partnership that led to a series of, well... some pretty "forging" fires.

The long practices, the brainstorming sessions, and the scrimmages all had varying levels of fieriness; but actually, competing was certainly the most scorching of them all, especially when there are shenanigans afoot.

At my first-ever mock trial regionals competition, we had a particularly interesting third (final) round. This round was crucial because we went up against a pretty good team and, if we didn't win, it could mean losing our chance at advancing to the state competition.

Because I was new to the team, I had one witness role, which meant that I only played on one side of the case. The side we played during this round was the one that I wasn't on, so I watched everything that transpired from a spectator's point of view.

Everything seemed well and good at first, but as we progressed further into the round, we started to notice some very peculiar choices from the other team. Some of their witnesses avoided our cross-examination questions and had some… *questionable* responses. Then, they tried impeaching one of our witnesses on something really, really stupid. Semantics! And then, when the judge asked how much time each side had remaining (both sides get an allotted time that is recorded by members of both teams), they had an enormous time discrepancy compared to what we had recorded.

This was some Slytherin *(Harry Potter)* antics, for sure.

The judge seemed confused and called both teams' timekeepers up to the bench. Spectators in the gallery whispered to one another, and the room was rife with suspense. I was sitting to the right of my coach's husband, and boy, were we fired up! We really felt that this team was playing dirty.

After a few minutes, the judge directed the timekeepers back to their seats and announced a new time—the median of the timekeeper's remaining times. This meant that, while we didn't proceed according to the other team's claim of time remaining, we had to make a compromise and lost a few minutes which, in mock trial, can severely impact the case.

The trial continued onward, and eventually, we reached closing arguments. Because we were on the Defense during this round, we would give our closing argument last. After the Prosecution finished theirs, our Defense "closer" began his closing argument and, about a third of the way through, the unexpected happened.

We got kicked out of the room! Because the competition coordinators were essentially "renting out" an entire public courthouse, everyone had to be out of it by a certain time. A woman burst through our courtroom door, halted the trial, and demanded everyone leave the building. Apparently, all of the extra time spent on objections to confusing statements, half-assed impeachments, and the timekeeping dilemma sent us past the all-stop time.

Our judge tried her best to plead with the woman, saying we needed just five more minutes. It was the closing argument, after all—the very last part of the trial. But there was no negotiating with the time. We *had* to get out.

As the entire courtroom stood up and scrambled to get their things together, the woman left and the judge told our "closer" to continue delivering his closing argument to the jury while we packed up. Under pressure, he sped up, but there wasn't enough time. He didn't get to finish.

How could we be scored fairly on our closing argument if it was interrupted? If he had to speed up his delivery and wasn't even able to finish?

I am sure it wouldn't surprise you if I told you that my team was absolutely *fuming*. We were pretty convinced that all of the shenanigans from the other team had resulted in our inability to finish our case. This wasn't fair, and my team was determined to get it rectified.

We sped down the bajillions of courthouse staircases, complaining, contemplating our next move, and perhaps even cursing throughout our descent (no, there was definitely cursing). We also decided our next move would be to contact the competition coordinator to get this figured out.

When we got to the first floor, we were herded outside and found the competition coordinator. We had some passionate words with her, and she let us know that, apparently, there was another team that was also interrupted in the middle of their trial.

We stood outside in the cold for fifteen minutes to a half hour, beat up from the long day, but empowered with the determination to amend this injustice (and lots of adrenaline). Then, the competition coordinator said they had a plan: They got permission to use two of the rooms at a different courthouse a few blocks away and that, while there, we could finish the rest of our trials.

So, we walked. No, actually, we *stomped* our way to the courthouse.

It wasn't that far, but getting there seemed like an eternity. Not quite the final ascent of Mt. Doom, but still very challenging. The stakes were too high not to obsess about it.

When we arrived, we waited in the lobby until the competition coordinator brought our "closer" in to finish his closing argument. The door shut, and he was gone for ten minutes or so. At this point, we were sure we had lost. The trial was so odd and we didn't look too good on some of those weird half-impeachments. We were ready to hear the worst.

When our "closer" finished, he walked out with a confident look—he thought it had gone well. Our coach caught the competition coordinator on her way out of the room and we were assured that all roles had been scored and the trial was complete. But the team didn't seem hopeful. We felt defeated.

We left the courthouse and headed to dinner. The results wouldn't be out until later that evening, and why not celebrate our hard work together no matter the result? We had a great time discussing everything that had happened throughout the competition with an emphasis on the absurdity of the last trial.

And what do you know? Half-way through dinner, the results were posted and we were pleased to find that we had made it to the state competition... and so did that team we went up against in that final round. But hey, we went on to beat them at the state competition, so it's all good.

Slytherin didn't get away with it!

All the time spent together, all the ways we helped each other deal with disappointments, and the movement toward our shared goal created that genuine connection and made us an incredible team.

If you guys are reading this—you know who you are—you mean more to me than you'll ever know. Stay safe!

By the time we were watching *Harry Potter* that day,
my Co-author had inserted some of the most beautiful,
compassionate, and strong allies a girl could ask for into
my storyline. They had all arrived in my life at just the
right moments with the messages, superpowers, and tools
I needed to take my next steps on my own healing journey.
Some of them left as soon as their purpose in my life was
complete; others have stayed and continued to walk the
journey alongside me. We take turns initiating connection,
sharing our resources, carrying each other's heavy loads, and
lending our superpowers to the bigger collective journey we
are all working to rewrite.

I can honestly say that I am terrified to think of where
I would be physically, emotionally, mentally, spiritually,
and professionally if not for these women and men. Their
presence in my life is some of the best evidence I have that
there is a Co-author who loves us so deeply that It's always
writing in new characters with new opportunities to remember who we really are and become true to our intention.
I know that, when I'm nearing the end of this story, their
faces, love, and contributions to my life are the treasure that I
will be taking with me.

I've prayed for Aaron to be blessed with the same type
of friendship fortune and my heart hurt to watch him feel
lonely, unseen, and even betrayed as he navigated some of
the same storylines I'd experienced as a child. I truly believe
that it was stories of epic friendships in *Harry Potter* and
Avatar: The Last Airbender that helped both of us to write

a new friendship story for ourselves. We also learned from time spent watching "friendships gone wrong" in other stories, exploring the roots of the misunderstandings and betrayals, and talking about whether they could have been saved and how.

Last year, I knew he, too, had struck gold when he came home and told me about how much fun he was having in mock trial and game nights with friends. Even though it meant lost hangout time for me, my heart was full of gratitude that he was beginning to experience the joy of working with others toward a common goal and just having fun with other brilliant souls on this journey.

Diving Deeper into Camaraderie
with Your Kids and Their Stories

We Need Each Other

Name a hero that saves the world by themself. That's right, you can't. Because it's simply not possible. When evil rises to power, through methods of deception and domination, it always grows to be more powerful than the individual hero. Making friends that have their back is not only vital to the hero's success, but in many cases, to their survival as well. How many times have you watched a hero almost die or become mortally wounded only to be saved by a close friend or ally? How about when Anna was turned into ice so she could save Elsa (*Frozen*), or when Aragorn and Arwen saved Frodo from the Nazgûl (*Lord of The Rings*)? Or even when Dobby saved Harry, Ron, and Hermione at Malfoy Manor (*Harry Potter*)? Through love and sacrifice, those with *true* friends will always fare better than those who try to go it alone.

Plus, history has repeatedly shown that alliances built on trust, friendship, and a righteous goal (as opposed to fear, control, and a lust for power) tend to be the ones that come out on top. This is also reflected in Harry Potter's close friendship with Hermione and Ron who are united against Voldemort and his loyal servants. Even though Harry almost always wanted to fight whatever evil arose by himself to keep his friends out of harm's way, Ron and Hermione *refused* to let him go alone.

As time goes on, even through betrayal and heartache, the bonds of friendship strengthen, especially after experiencing the hardship that comes with the trials and tribulations that companions face. What matters most, however, is that they face them together.

Which of your child's favorite stories is friendship-focal?

How can you help your child connect the "sense of belonging" between those characters to their own experience of, or desire for, the same feeling of connection and companionship?

Belonging is one of our most basic primal needs. We truly do need the experience of connection, safety, and trust in relationship to thrive in the world; and we will unconsciously seek it at every turn. When we have conversations about this basic need and ask children to identify how it shows up in the characters and stories, we help them begin to identify it in themselves. Instead of being unconsciously driven to experience belonging, children will be able to consciously choose *with whom* they truly belong.

Choosing vs. Accepting Friendship

Have you noticed that villains are always lonely? We're not talking about the kind of loneliness you feel when you're bored or when there's nobody around to talk to. We're talking about the kind of loneliness you feel when you have nobody to lean on, no friends to confide in, and no reciprocal exchange of love. Naturally, many villains have "followers" that do their bidding and pretend to show admiration and devotion, but have you noticed that those followers tend to do those things out of fear of being castigated? Maybe if they don't agree to help the villain, their wealth will be taken away, or a goal of theirs thwarted? Maybe there's a threat of serious harm to their loved ones, themselves, or worse? That isn't friendship. Not *true* friendship, at least.

In *Harry Potter and The Order of the Phoenix*, after an intense battle, Harry says to Voldemort, "You're the one who is weak. You will never know love or friendship. And I feel sorry for you." This shows that Harry knows that he has true friends, as opposed to Voldemort, and that he is stronger than him because of that.

In contrast, Zuko, one of the main villains in *Avatar: The Last Airbender*, is surrounded by family members that pretend like they love each other to get what they want. In reality, they're competing for power within the family while they force their power on the rest of the world. Zuko eventually joins the Avatar and his companions (Team Avatar!) not only because he sees the generational wrongdoings of his family and how his decisions have caused pain, but also because he recognized and wanted the real love and friendship he'd had with his mother before she had to escape from his father's tyrannical family.

Friends who *choose* to be our friends are the ones that we can count on. They're often loyal, honest, and caring, while those who *accept* friendship out of fear, greed, spite, or other reasons without any motive to love or support, may abandon us when things get tough, ignore requests for help, and even betray us.

> *Which of your child's favorite characters embody this chosen friendship — those indestructible bonds?*

> *How can you draw your child's attention to the difference between accepting/tolerating a friendship that has been thrust upon them and choosing someone to be their confidant and ally?*

The truth is the chances are high that we will find ourselves in situations where we have to be and work with people we may not naturally choose as friends, and it's important to help children prepare for that. Identifying characters who are able to not just show tolerance and acceptance, but who use curiosity, humor, or some other quality to find common ground can spark conversations around how your child can do this throughout their lives. Our favorite story of this dynamic shift is between Gimli and Legolas in *Lord of The*

Rings. They started out as enemies, but they were ready to die side-by-side as friends.

We truly believe that small shifts into curiosity made in our individual relationships is the only truly sustainable way to co-create and preserve a world where we stop labeling and excluding people for the cultural, racial, socioeconomic, sexual, and other identities that we simply do not understand.

Teamwork and Strengths

In many epic stories, the friends that join the hero usually conveniently need to use their unique skills, knowledge, and personalities to complete the tasks at hand or simply survive the darkness that wishes to destroy them. Harry, Ron, and Hermione (*Harry Potter*) are a great example of this. They needed to leverage each other's strengths to come out victorious: Harry's curiosity and courage, Hermione's intellect and wisdom, and Ron's easy-going and level-headed personality. SImilarly, Aang, Sokka, Katara, Toph, Zuko, and others (*Avatar: The Last Airbender*) use their unique knowledge and abilities to fight an enemy with various fighting strategies, clear an obstacle that only an earth-bender can destroy, convince old acquaintances to fight alongside them, and other tests or adversities.

That's not to say that companions don't have their liabilities. In fact, some may screw up... a lot. Take Neville Longbottom (*Harry Potter*), for instance. At the beginning of the series, even though he was a great friend, he was mostly a clumsy character that caused more trouble than he put to rest. In the last part of the series, he wields the Sword of Gryffindor and delivers one of the final blows to Voldemort's soul by killing Voldemort's snake. In *The Lord of the Rings*, Merry Brandybuck and Pippin Took had a very similar proclivity for causing trouble, even with their best intentions. However, in *The Two Towers*, they successfully rallied the Ents and Huorns of Fangorn Forest to destroy the lair of Saruman the White. They also went on to play important roles in *The Return of the King*. In *Avatar: The Last Airbender*, even though Sokka wasn't nearly as clumsy or troublesome as the last two examples were, he made his fair share of mistakes. Later, he learned the art of the sword and became a fearsome (but still loveable) foe.

And sometimes, the people heroes need with them on their journey aren't easy to get along with. Just like real life, huh? In the beginning of *Brother Bear,* Kenai, the main character, doesn't want to have anything to do with Koda, a young friend that proves to be annoying at times. However, he stays with him in order to achieve his goal and eventually realizes that their journey was meant to be taken together — for both of their benefit.

In which of your children's favorite stories do you see friends intentionally using their superpowers to achieve their goal?

How can you help them identify each of the characters' strengths and how working together compensates for their separate weaknesses and helps them achieve their goals faster?

How many times have you felt like you have to figure it all out on your own and gone in circles trying to find answers? Of course, we are not just talking about tasks and activities in these superpower conversations; we are also talking about qualities and characteristics that seem more natural or developed for some folks than others. This is where we can deepen our curiosities and conversations with our children around "What is it about that character's nature and nurture that makes them so good at _____?" and explore strength in diversity of culture and experience. Truly, treat this as an opportunity to discover which cultures tend to be more communal and which are more individualistic, spiritual and materialistic, artistic and calculative, etc., and have conversations about the strengths of each and how, with a little curiosity and communication, we might be able to work alongside each other more powerfully to make this world a better place.

Sacrifice

The concept that we must sacrifice what we have today so that we can make the future better is an especially important one in many stories and how we live our lives. In the real world, you probably do things like save money over a long period of time rather than spending it all at once so that you have enough money for an emergency or when you retire. But in certain situations and stories full of adventure and danger, sacrifice often takes a much more serious role. Heroes are sometimes required to act selflessly if they want to save their loved ones or help their camarades to complete their quest. It almost seems to be a law of nature or a part of the human condition that in the end, their sacrifice is almost never made in vain.

In *Harry Potter and the Deathly Hallows*, Severus Snape, previously suspected by Harry and his friends to be a villain, gave his life for the well-being of the people he cared for. His sacrifice prevented Voldemort from obtaining the Elder Wand (the most powerful wand ever created), which ultimately helped those who sought to thwart Voldemort and his followers. Then there was Katniss Everdeen (*Hunger Games*), who volunteered to replace her little sister who had been chosen at random to compete in the Hunger Games — an event where children fight to the death for entertainment and "glory." In *Frozen*, Anna was turned into ice after stepping in front of Elsa, thereby saving her from the same fate. Princess Yue of the Northern Water Tribe (*Avatar: The Last Airbender*) gave her life to the Moon Spirit to save the world from imbalance and the ongoing attack of the fire nation. In *Brother Bear*, the eldest brother Sitka used his spear to fracture a cliff of ice and start an avalanche that stopped the bear that was trying to kill his younger brothers, but he also ended his own life.

Villains sacrifice things, too, but never in the same ways or for the same selfless reasons as heroes. In *Harry Potter and the Half-Blood Prince*, we find out that when Voldemort was younger, he killed many people to split his soul into "horcruxes," to make it extremely difficult for someone to kill him. In *Game of Thrones,* it didn't take much for Melisandre to convince Stannis Baratheon to sacrifice his own daughter in the hopes of protecting his army and his perceived claim to the Iron Throne. In other words, heroes tend to sacrifice themselves to reach their goals while villains sacrifice others.

Which of your children's favorite stories and characters would give you the opportunity to talk about the temptations of conformity for belonging?

What does healthy compromise and sacrifice in friendships look and feel like?

Because of that deep need for belonging, we can unconsciously begin to sacrifice or compromise parts of ourselves that we feel make us different or unacceptable to certain individuals or groups. It's a survival instinct, and it shouldn't surprise us that children find themselves in situations where they are being asked to try or do things that don't feel right or true to them and do them anyway. The need to belong is simply that strong.

What if we explored this with children through stories and then made connections to their own experiences of wanting to belong? What if we asked them to begin to define their boundaries around what they are willing to do and not willing to do for that experience of belonging *before* they were offered an opportunity to prove themselves worthy of a particular group? What if we asked them what they feel healthy sacrifice for someone we love looks like, and where or how it could become unhealthy? Well, we believe that if we do this early with our children, we empower them to preserve their individuality and sense of worth as well as more clearly identify the individuals and groups to which they *want to belong.*

Forged in Fire

You probably have friendships that were created under all kinds of circumstances, but the ones that were "forged in fire," or created under strenuous circumstances, are likely some of the closest and longest-lasting friendships you have. It might be a "strenuous circumstance" such as Mock Trial competitions that rely on adaptability, performance, and teamwork. There's nothing like walking into the pressure of a competition and walking out of it with a sense of accomplishment that was earned through hard work and collaboration with friends. Perhaps it is collaborating with other entrepreneurs on a massive project in which everyone can win, and then having to navigate all of the challenges that arise along the way... together. These types of experiences are reflected to us in many of our favorite stories.

Throughout the *Harry Potter* series, Harry, Ron, and Hermione are regularly found working together in dangerous circumstances and under immense stress, whether that be outwitting a mountain troll in the girl's lavatory, secretly teaching students how to defend themselves despite the commands of a tyrannical headmaster, or working together to defeat the greatest dark wizard of all time. In *Avatar: The Last Airbender*, Team Avatar works together to stop the Fire Nation from destroying the world. Of course, one of the most epic examples of friendships (almost literally) forged in fire is that of Frodo and Sam (*The Lord of The Rings*) who are frequently faced with trials and tribulations that are occasionally so overwhelming they almost give up and return home. Over time, these friendships grow stronger and stronger so they may survive the tests, obstacles, and dark powers they will face. Two friends, who had survived such a long and tumultuous journey, were able to resist the seductive force of the One Ring.

Even those that you might suspect would never become friends find themselves experiencing brotherly love or chummy admiration. In the beginning of *The Lord of the Rings* trilogy, Legolas the elf and Gimli the dwarf spout passive-aggressive comments toward each other; and after months of fighting wars together, they end up as friends in the final battle where Gimli teases Legolas, "I never thought I'd die fighting side-by-side with an Elf."

Legolas smiles and says, "What about side-by-side with a friend?"

"Aye. I could do that," Gimli agrees.

Sometimes friendships are strengthened through how they decide to cope with the weight of the world. In *Harry Potter and the Deathly Hallows*, Harry and Hermione dance to forget for a moment that Ron had left them after a disagreement and the Dark Lord was trying to kill them. Merry and Pippin (*The Lord of The Rings*) keep hectic situations light by cracking jokes and indulging in delicious food. We see the same thing with Legolas and Gimli, again, when they start competing and shout at each other (mid-battle, mind you) how many enemies they've killed. As Gimli is swinging his axe in the Battle of Helm's Deep, he clamors from atop the wall, "Twenty! Twenty-one!" That line gets us every time.

How can you help your child make the connection here between Uncertainty and Camaraderie?

What is it about facing Uncertainty with allies that makes it more tolerable at some times and more challenging at others?

This is what we all want — allies who will not only support us toward our individual and collective goals, but who will do so when we need it the most. This is an excellent opportunity to talk about the qualities and superpowers of friends that would support our child the most, including the ability to self-regulate and stay the course even when faced with uncertainty. This is not about holding an impossible standard of perfection; it's about helping children identify the qualities of a real friend who they can trust to stand by them through life's inevitable challenges.

Intentional vs. Accidental Betrayal

Tales of betrayal are important teachers that show us how we can identify loyalty, or lack thereof, in those that we call our friends, as well as how we should confront the inevitable misunderstandings and mistakes that can occur in our friendships.

A foundation of loyalty is established when people choose friendship rather than accept it. Again, choosing friendship means that we are agreeing to a friendship at our own discretion for reasons that are genuine, while accepting friendship means that we are being pressured into a relationship for survival or fear of what might happen if we don't.

Intentional betrayal is usually carried out by someone that accepted friendship, betrayed themselves, or initiated a false friendship with someone for personal gain. For example, in *The Matrix*, Cypher betrayed Neo and the rest of the crew in exchange for the luxuries that he missed in the matrix. "Ignorance is bliss," right? Gollum (*The Lord of The Rings*) felt betrayed by Sam and Frodo after they were captured by Faramir and decided to destroy Sam and Frodo's friendship. When that didn't work, he tried feeding Frodo to Shelob the spider so that he could take the One Ring for himself.

Friends can accidentally betray one another, too, creating a divide between them. Have you ever made a choice, rooted in a misunderstanding, that indirectly and negatively impacted one of your friends? You didn't do it to harm them on purpose, but it might have taken some time for your friend to forgive you. In *Brother Bear*, Koda feels betrayed when he finds out that Kenai was partly responsible for his mother's death. He didn't know and probably didn't care that Kenai had hunted Koda's mother because he thought that she ate their fish and destroyed their basket. When they physically confronted her, they didn't realize that she was only trying to protect her child. When Aang (*Avatar: The Last Airbender*) ran away from his responsibility as the Avatar, he got caught in a storm that nearly killed him and, using his Avatar powers, he froze himself in ice for one-hundred years. As a result, the Air Nation had to defend themselves from the Fire Nation without the help of the Avatar, and was destroyed. When Aang finally emerged from the ice, he felt as though it was his fault that the Air Nation had been wiped out because he had accidentally abandoned them in their time of need.

In many cases, the events leading up to perceived betrayals are orchestrated by those who would wish to turn their allies against each other and weaken them. In *The Lion King*, in a plot to claim the throne as his own, Scar intentionally betrayed his brother, Mufasa, and his nephew, Simba. Consequently, Simba accidentally betrayed his own people by leaving and renouncing his claim to the throne because Scar convinced him that *he* was the reason his father died and that nobody would accept him back. Simba ran away from his kingdom and his people because he didn't view himself as worthy, and in doing so, left his people at the mercy of his traitorous uncle, Scar.

Fortunately, many betrayals can be reconciled.

*What stories provide you with an opportunity
to discuss betrayal and explore the difference
between misunderstandings or accidents
and more malicious experiences?*

*Were there any signs of malicious intent or plotting?
If so, what were those red flags that the
character (and we) should watch for?*

When we talk about empowering children to preserve their freedom, cultivating this level of discernment is vital. If we can help them identify indicators of malintent and stay attuned as they develop relationships, they can promptly remove themselves from potentially dangerous situations, be more clever about how they navigate the relationship, and/or confront problems more directly. They can also be more prepared to deal with those accidental betrayals and give their friends those generous assumptions that they were probably doing the best they could and simply made a mistake.

Restoration of Trust
Reconciling betrayal is probably one of the most important things we can learn how to do for ourselves and those we love, and good stories show us how. Accidental betrayals are hard to forgive, and intentional betrayals are excruciatingly difficult to redeem. After a betrayal, we wonder how we could ever trust again? When we make a mistake that manifests a misunderstanding, how do we make it up to the people that we love? How do we restore the trust that we so carefully cultivated and later shattered with a choice that we regret? Whether we are the one who suffered the betrayal of a friend, or the one who accidentally hurt someone we love, reconciliation requires the same elements: consistent corrective action, sincere words, and every so often, lots of time.

In *Harry Potter and the Deathly Hallows*, Ron became suspicious, and later jealous, of Harry and Hermione's relationship. He loved Hermione and became upset when he thought she was falling in love with Harry. In combination with the emotionally and mentally manipulative locket that Ron was wearing, he felt betrayed and got so angry that he left. When he had cooled off, he returned in time to save Harry from drowning in the lake where he was retrieving a sword important to their mission (consistent corrective action). They walked back to their camp where a frustrated Hermione yelled at Ron for leaving. When she finally allowed him to speak, Ron told the story of what had happened after he left and about the events and strange forces that brought him back to his best friends (sincere words). Hermione was somewhat moved by the story, but still hurt that Ron had left in the first place. Over time, she forgave him and began to trust him again (lots of time).

Kenai apologized to Koda (*Brother Bear*) for being involved with his mother's death and told the story of what happened (sincere words). At the end of the story, Kenai chose not to return as a human and instead remained in the form of a bear to look over the orphaned bear (consistent corrective action). In *Avatar: The Last Airbender*, because of his accidental betrayal of the Air Nation (and arguably the world), he worked tirelessly to become the best Avatar ever (consistent corrective action). He traveled to various nations to apologize to the people that were affected, as well as assisted them with their problems (sincere words and corrective action). In time, he restored balance to the world and earned back their trust (lots of time).

In *The Lion King*, Simba returned to Pride Rock and led the demise of Scar (consistent corrective action). During this final encounter with Scar, Simba told the story of the events that led to his departure and how Scar had manipulated him and the kingdom for power (sincere words). When Gollum framed Sam (*The Lord of The Rings*) and accused him of eating the little food they had left for their journey, Frodo believed him and told Sam to leave. After finding evidence that he had been framed, Sam went back and ended up saving Frodo from Shelob the spider and the orcs of Mordor (consistent corrective action). Through the act of saving Frodo's life, Sam proved again that he was sincere and dedicated to seeing his friend through to the end of the journey.

While it may be tough, forgiving those who accidentally betray us is important not only for the sake of our friendships, but for our own well-being. Knowing who is loyal to us and especially *why* they're loyal to us is an invaluable awareness. Being willing to compromise and apologize for the potential unforeseen negative consequences of our actions will help us keep our relationships intact and healthy. As the heroes of our own lives, we must seek out and *choose* friendships and alliances that support us and our mission, are there of their own volition and mutually ready to sacrifice, will endure discord and learn to forgive accidents and misunderstandings, and are built on love, loyalty, and trust.

In which stories do you see healthy repairs of relationships — heartfelt apologies and careful amends (actions) that restore trust over time?

How could you point out and explore the steps, elements, and qualities of healthy repair?

As Carl Jung said, "We don't get wounded alone, and we don't heal alone." If we can prepare children to leverage the strengths and navigate the kryptonite of their allies, and celebrate collaboration and make repairs when it all goes wrong, we can increase their capacity for meaning and happiness in every area of their life. Relationships with friends, romantic partners, colleagues, bosses/clients, etc. will all be a whole lot easier and more joyful.

Chapter Five

Redemption

"I revoke my curse! Let it be no more!"

~ Maleficent ~

The ache in my chest started when I saw her watery eyes staring through the window at Aurora's sleeping body, but it exploded when she walked into the room and began chanting, "I revoke my curse! Let it be no more!"

As I watched her conjure every ounce of power and intention to undo what she had done, tears of regret streamed down my face as I remembered that terrible day. Aaron continued to watch the movie while I disappeared into a bad scene from our story. The long line in the small department store. The stuffed animal and his overly-tired, two-year-old begging that escalated into a full tantrum. The flush of humiliation that I couldn't afford such a small toy, and the immediate projection of that shame onto his behavior. The nearly-blacked-out rage that took over as I grabbed him at his elbow, dragged him across the parking lot, and hurled him into his car seat with too much force.

144 A Religion of Story

The wrestling match and the spanking. His tearful, horrified expression, and the lack of recognition of the person who had birthed and cared for him. And then the same feeling I saw in Maleficent's eyes — absolutely overwhelming regret and the question: *Oh my God, what have I done?!? Will I ever be able to undo this?*

I blinked my eyes as the memory faded and looked over at my son as he reclined on the couch. Noticing the inflammation that had emerged in his little body over the last year, I wondered how much of that was my doing.

Turning my attention back to the movie, I watched as Maleficent hopelessly pondered the future of this young girl who she'd cursed before she had the opportunity to know and love her. My heart broke a little when Aurora realized that it was Maleficent who had cursed her and ran toward her fate. We held our breath as, despite all of her father's and Maleficent's attempts to protect her from her cursed fate, Aurora found her way to her demise. Like most viewers, we were stunned when the prince's kiss didn't wake her from her enchanted state.

"Mom, why didn't it work?" he asked.

"I don't know? Maybe it's Diablo? He's always loved her since she was little?" I asked no one in particular.

Just then, Maleficent walked over to Aurora's bedside and whispered, "I will not ask your forgiveness because what I have done to you is unforgivable. I was so lost in hatred and revenge. Sweet Aurora, you stole what was left of my heart. And now I've lost you forever. I swear, no harm will come to you as long as I live. And not a day shall pass that I don't miss your smile."

When she bent down to kiss her on her forehead, I knew. *OMGoodness, of course! It's her!*

"Wow!" Aaron turned to look at me, his eyes wide. He knew, even at eight years old, that he was witnessing a major departure from the typical Disney storyline.

"No truer love," says Diablo as the two women embrace.

I waited until the movie was over to discuss what we had just witnessed and I'm glad we did because Disney served up even more in the last ten minutes. Maleficent found her wings, chose not to kill the king at the end of the battle, and then tore down the thorns she had built up around her kingdom.

So symbolic of what she had done with her own heart after she had been wounded. Wow, this is amazing!

I gasped a little as the narrator, Aurora, closed the film: "In the end, my kingdom was united not by a hero or a villain, as legend had predicted, but by one who was both hero and villain."

Wow. Both hero and villain. So much truer to real life.

I turned off the tv and he sat up and looked at me, ready for a conversation.

"So, this was really different from the old story of *Sleeping Beauty,* wasn't it?" I started.

"Yes!" He nodded and waited for me to continue.

"What was different?" I put the question back to him, to give him the opportunity to connect some of the dots on his own.

"Well, in this one, we found out *why* Maleficent was evil. She was hurt by someone she loved and became lost in hatred and revenge, like she said."

"Exactly. And did that make you feel any differently about this Maleficent than you did about the one in *Sleeping Beauty?*"

He took a moment to reflect on his feelings. "Yes, I did feel differently about this one. I wanted her to..." He paused, searching for the right word. "...Be better... to stop being a 'bad guy'... to find a way to undo the curse and be friends with Aurora again."

"Yeah, I felt like I was cheering for the villain as much as I was for Aurora, and that seems like a new experience." Aaron nodded in agreement while my mind searched for other villains. *Ohhh.* "But maybe it's not? I've rooted for two other villains, come to think of it. In *Star Wars,* there was a 'dark side' character that you were hoping would somehow find their way back to the right side of The Force."

"Yes, Anakin!"

"Right! In that last episode when he is going to the dark side and doing terrible things, I kept hoping that he would change all the way to the end when he has the opportunity to save Luke." I nodded to let him know that I thought we were on to something. "And what about *Avatar*? Which character — "

"Zuko!" he exclaimed. "He is a bad guy right up 'til the last season, and then he has a change of heart."

"Hmmm... interesting. What does this make you wonder about other 'bad guys' or 'villains' in other movies?"

He reflected for a moment quietly. "It makes me want to ask, 'Who hurt you?'" He said it with a genuinely concerned look on his face that turned into a grin.

"Right. I actually really like this new approach to stories. It makes more sense in real life, doesn't it? I mean, I've never thought that people were just born to be bad. The people who have been villains in my life have all suffered a ton of abuse or pain. And I know that I've done terrible things because of my own pain. It's good to see the movies are starting to show that some villains can be redeemed." He tilted his head to let me know that he didn't understand the new word. "Redeemed means that they can be saved, too. They can find their way back to the good side." He nodded in understanding. "But it's not easy... I mean, think about what Zuko had to go through to leave the dark side and then prove himself worthy of Team Avatar."

"Yeah, they didn't trust him at all. He had to keep doing the right thing and apologizing when he made mistakes."

"That's how we all come back from mistakes, isn't it? We have to apologize and then prove that we are changed inside by behaving better on the outside. Maleficent had the opportunity to continue being a villain when she had the king trapped, but she didn't kill him. She was trying to walk away."

"Makes sense. Better choices. More hero-like choices," he surmised.

"Maybe it just takes more time for people who have traveled further into the dark side?" I let the question hang in the air between us.

"Yes, some villains seem too evil, like Voldemort, but maybe there was a chance for him at some point..." He looked down at the ground, deep in contemplation.

Realizing that he was approaching his limit, I wrapped up the conversation. "Well, it's a very new idea. I say we think about it and pick this up again later. Let's go make some dinner."

Redemption

- What did you learn about good and evil, and heroes and villains, from your favorite childhood movies, tv series, and books? Did you assume that they were born bad, or did you wonder how the bad guys became so evil? Did the stories you engaged explain the villain's backstory, so that you understood their naughty behavior? Did it ever occur to you that the villain could come back from the dark side, or did you just write them off and assume their fate was predetermined?

I honestly cannot remember a story from my childhood in which I saw a compelling backstory for a villain like the one we saw in *Maleficent*, but I know that I at least saw a big spectrum of villainry (yes, it's a new word). There were the pure evil villains like the Queen Grimhilde character in *Snow White* and The Wicked Witch of the West in *The Wizard of Oz;* but there were also the (arguably) less destructive (and obviously terrified) tyrannical fathers in *Footloose* and *Dirty Dancing* and the vengeful souls in the soap operas I watched with my aunt over summer vacations.

But what struck me as I looked back at the list of my all-time favorite stories was the pattern of the villain being an elusive/deceptive dark force or institution and/or the idea of blindly conforming to that force/institution. As a very little one, I was so mad at "the government" (whoever they were!) for interfering with Elliot and E.T.'s friendship (*E.T.*) and The Nothing that overtook the magical world of Fantasia (*The Neverending Story*). Then there was the father in *Footloose* — the pastor who set ridiculously high standards for his daughter, his congregation, and his community. No dancing?!?!? I mean, come on! His controlling behavior and dismissal of his daughter's desires upset me, but it was the words and actions of his congregants that really pissed me off. I understood by the end of the story that he was driven by his fear of losing another loved one to death or hell, but his blind "disciples" never questioned what they were told. Backstories, and understanding the psychology of the villain, definitely made a difference to me.

It also turns out that two of my "Top 5" movies both villainized conformity and the forces that drive it. The scene that impacted me the most the first time I watched *Dead Poets Society* was the one in which Robin William's character asks three students to walk around a small courtyard in front of their peers. In a short time, they fell into step with each other and marched lockstep while their peers clapped in unison until he stopped them and explained, "I brought them up here to illustrate the point of conformity — the difficulty of maintaining your own beliefs in the face of others'... We all have a great need for acceptance, but you must trust that your beliefs are unique, your own, though others may think them odd or unpopular... I want you to find your own walk." A few years later, I sat riveted by a similar message in *The Matrix* as Morpheus explained, "The Matrix is a system, Neo. That system is our enemy. But when you're inside, you look around, what do you see? Businessmen, teachers, lawyers, carpenters. The very minds of the people we are trying to save... It is the world that has been pulled over your eyes to blind you from the truth." In *Dead Poets Society*, the villain is the educational institution that demands conformity and compliance from its students and teachers. In *The Matrix*, it's a control program, its makers, and the agents of unconsciousness that protect it. As I was reflecting on all of this, I thought, *Is it any wonder that my personal and professional life are consumed with helping people retain independence of thought and speech in a world that tends to worship order over chaos, and in bodies designed to adapt and co-regulate to maintain a sense of safety and belonging?*

Now that you have identified some of the patterns in your early villain exposure, do you see any commonalities between the villains you watched in stories and those that have appeared in your life?

There are the *obvious* villains — the ones with the menacing stares and wicked laughs who appear to be mostly unredeemable. But what if, like me, you grew up not realizing that every villain does not look and sound evil — that some actually show up like heroes — and/or you knew *why* some of them "behave badly"?

In my experience, this has resulted in either not seeing or willfully ignoring "villain tells," a term Aaron coined to explain the varied expressions, tones, and strategic moves of villains. In some cases, I just didn't realize that I was dealing with a darksider and got swept up by their charisma or cause and then found myself bullied, beaten up, or betrayed. (This is exactly what had happened to me just before *Maleficent* found its way onto my tv screen.) In other relationships, I knew they had been deeply wounded, so I made excuses for their bad behavior because I also saw the potential for redemption and tried to save them. I haven't dealt with any obvious or purely evil villains in my life; the ones I've faced have been abused souls who had big charisma and a superpower that made it hard for me to believe that they had anything else but my best interest at heart. Over the years, they've all taught me the same lesson: When someone is in pain, and doesn't have the awareness to see it or the tools to process it, they really only have one goal — to prevent more personal suffering — and will do almost anything to reach it.

After a few run-ins with villains, I started to make a list of those "villain tells," so now I can see them coming and set appropriate boundaries (or run). I've also deepened my commitment to process old pain so that I don't accidentally become one, like a few of the people I have loved and lost... and like that shame-ridden mommy who destroyed her son's sense of safety so many years ago. Engaging great stories is one way that I've been able to sort this out with Aaron by my side. The two of us have spent a lot of time arguing about the exact moments when heroes become villains and villains become heroes.

She was Both, and I Loved Her

"So this is how you treat me after all I've done for you?!" she shrieked.

I watched in horror as my great-grandmother reacted to us telling her the news. After my parents had devoted five years to helping her as her health declined, we had decided to move out of state.

And she was *not* happy about it.

"Gramma, it's time for us to go. But we are leaving you in really good hands..." My mom continued to fill her in on all of the details as Gramma withdrew/collapsed into herself at the head of the table, her arms crossed and brow furrowed. We had been preparing to have this conversation for a while, knowing that there was no universe where it would be easy.

My mom finished saying her piece and stared intently at Gramma, waiting for a response. Instead of a reply, we sat in silence as Gramma stared at the table, tears streaming underneath her glasses and down her cheeks. My mom, dad, Theddee (a family friend and Gramma's caregiver at the time), and I occasionally glanced at one another exchanging pursed lips and raised eyebrows to deal with the tense and somber situation. This certainly wasn't going the way we hoped it would.

After using a few tissues and ten minutes or so of crying, Gramma abruptly stood up from her chair, grabbed her walker, and sobbed her way down the hall into her den.

After breathing a collective sigh of relief, Theddee stood up and followed.

The days following that conversation and leading up to the move were no easier. They were full of cold shoulders, loud sighs, tears, the silent treatment, and perhaps worst of all, impossible questions.

"Why are you doing this to me?"

"Why couldn't you move somewhere closer? Why are you leaving the state?"

"Don't you love me?"

After being inundated with these questions and watching her behavior, I started to see a different person. This person who I had lived with and loved my whole life began to guilt trip us at every turn. My playful, generous, and loving great-grandmother had become dimmed by her past, her pain, her fears, and her cognitive decline.

She became the manipulative Mother Gothel to our Rapunzel (*Tangled*). We knew she loved us, and we loved her, too. But when it came time to live our lives—to seek adventure and pave our own path—*we* became *her* villains.

As hard as it was to accept, she, too, had become an unexpected villain of my story. And I wanted to rewrite it.

Fast-forward ten months, I got the opportunity to fly by myself from our new home near Portland, Oregon, down to Southern California for my birthday. I was so excited to see my family that I hadn't been with in so long. That included Gramma, even though we didn't leave on the best of terms.

It was very late, and I had just deboarded my plane at Ontario Airport. I claimed my belongings and headed outside where I was picked up by Theddee. She had been taking care of Gramma full-time for the last year and gave me a warm greeting. Even though it had only been a year, it was surreal driving the familiar streets.

After fifteen minutes, we were greeted with the wall of hedges, olive trees sick with disease, and the grand wooden double-doors that guarded the entrance of my childhood home. We pulled into the driveway and into the garage.

I remember...

We had said our final goodbyes in this garage. I could still see Gramma standing in front of the tower of boxes, wiping away her tears.

It felt odd sleeping in the living room. It had barely changed. The couches were the same old—dusty but sturdy—and the wall of glass doll cabinets was glowing just the same. I never realized how creepy that cabinet was until that moment.

The night passed and I woke up to greet Gramma for the first time in what felt like forever. We didn't really talk on the phone—her hearing issues made it hard on her. All I knew was what I had heard from my mom who talked to Theddee regularly, and that was that she wasn't doing very well since we left.

I headed straight for her room, through the kitchen, the den, down the hallway, and as I approached, I could hear her talking to Theddee. She sounded just as I remembered.

I hung a left through the door and saw her perched upright in her bed. She had her morning toast lying in her lap and coffee in hand. It took her a moment to recognize what was happening, but as soon as she did, she lit right up. She was so happy to see me, and I was relieved. After everything that had happened leading up to our departure, I wasn't so sure I would be welcomed with such warmth as I had been.

Let me tell you, her bear hugs hadn't changed one bit. In fact, she may have misaligned more bones and ligaments than she normally did even though I was experienced in how to brace myself.

Even more odd, however, was her fascination with our new lives. She wanted to know everything, and I was glad to divulge. I told her the truth—we were feeling the best that we had ever felt in our lives—and that didn't seem to faze her. I think she had finally come to terms with our decision.

That isn't to say that she was a new person—oh, no—she was the same old Gramma in almost every other way. Her routine was the same, her refusal to let people help her was still very much alive, and her near-obsession with a pristinely clean house permeated every spotless corner and crevice of the downstairs area.

The day consisted of us relaxing, making good food, watching television, and tending to the garden. I listened to her talk about her diminished hearing and vision for about the third time that day as we made our way out of the house and into the pool area. As we walked past her pots, she joked about how she didn't need to wash them anymore because she didn't have dogs that peed on them all the time.

Good. Now we don't have to worry about her losing her balance and tripping over the hose every week.

She unlocked the gate to the pool next to the bar and guided me to the bench swing that was suspended from the ceiling. Overlooking the entire pool area, it was one of my favorite spots on the property.

We held hands as we stared at the calm water shimmering in the California sun. After some time, she let out a sigh. "Oh, Aaron, Aaron, Aaron." I looked at her intently. "I don't know how much longer I can keep this up."

Immediately, I knew what she meant. Life was getting harder for her to live. I remember thinking, *This is probably the last time I'm going to see her.* I scooched in closer to her and squeezed her hand, consciously capturing this moment in my memory as our last.

And sadly, it was. But I'm so grateful that I got to remember her this way. Joyful and full of love, even after all that we had put her through. And it was still easy to love her after all that she had put *us* through, too. We were able to look past our scars and remember what mattered most. We left each other not as villains, but as flawed people on our own journeys.

Whew. That story. Take a minute and grab a tissue if you need it. I know I have every time I've read it. What a powerful demonstration of the truth that we all have the potential to be heroes and villains, and how love and time heal. I really believe that it was the conversations we had about Maleficent and other villains who had become so because of their wounds that made this all possible.

If I've already said this a million times in this book, let me say it again: My Co-Author writes in the PERFECT stories at the perfect times. While Aaron was working on his parts of this chapter, the show *Lucifer* crossed my path. So, he kept writing, and I snuggled into bed and binge-watched a redemption story about a character that, by all accounts, has been considered the worst villain in history.

Interesting, right? It got me thinking again: Why is this whole villain redemption story a new trend in our culture? I believe that it's because we, as a society, are waking up to the truth that we are complex creatures that wield the capacity to both create and destroy. While most of us prefer to think of ourselves as mostly-good folks who want to do mostly-good things, it is true that we all are always just an impulsive word or action away from unleashing darkness and destruction. Most of us have told lies, taken scrupulous shortcuts, and acted selfishly to the pain and detriment of others and/or ourselves. We know, intuitively, that we could be just like that villain if just the right button is pushed at just the wrong time. And we all want to believe that part of us can be redeemed, especially if it has already raised its ugly head and done damage.

And with that awareness, we can have more compassion AND discernment. Compassion for those who are walking the hard path home to themselves and truth and compassion for ourselves as we strive to redeem our worst moments and most wounded parts. And discernment for those who are pretending to do so, or pretending that they already have achieved it. Aaron's term "villain tells" is literally the most important thing we can all take away from this chapter because, in a world where narratives can be manipulated by storytellers, journalists, and politicians, it's possible that the people being put before us as heroes are actually villains, and those we've been told are the worst villains ever might just be the ones saving the world.

Diving Deeper into Redemption with Your Kids and Their Stories

Who Hurt You?

There's a common theme that begins to reveal itself when we really look at how villains are created. And I'm not just talking about villains in movies and tv shows, but in real life, too. Although the particular circumstances that make otherwise "normal" individuals into villains are somewhat diverse, the one thing that most villains have in common is that they have experienced tremendous fear and/or pain.

Fear is a powerful force that can be used to persuade, control, and manipulate. A perfect example of this is the story of Anakin Skywalker's (*Star Wars*) transition to Darth Vader. Anakin saw visions of his pregnant wife, Princess Amidala, dying in childbirth. He feared her death, so he became obsessed with preventing it from happening; and when he was promised by the Supreme Chancellor that he could wield the power to stop her death, he caved to the teachings of the dark side to attain it. The road to hell is paved with good intentions, eh?

Other examples include *Frozen* and *Fantastic Beasts and Where to Find Them*, where the villain's fears take other forms. For instance, Credence (*Fantastic Beasts*) was forced to suppress his magic for fear of being ostracized by his anti-witchcraft family and friends. He beat himself up for his powers and tried to suppress them, but that only resulted in him opening himself up to be corrupted by a demonic dark force that drove him to cause destruction. When Elsa (*Frozen*) accidentally hurt her little sister with her ice powers, she became afraid that she might hurt other people she loved, so she tried to hide away and "conceal" herself. While Elsa never became an actual villain, one might argue that she easily could have turned into a lonely, bitter queen if not for her little sister's love and forgiveness.

The other part of the villain equation is pain. Pain can manifest as many things like loss, hardship, or other forms of suffering; and oftentimes, it will even evolve into rage. In *Maleficent*, her wings were cut off and taken by a man that later became king because of this accomplishment. This betrayal resulted not only in extreme physical pain, but the loss of her identity and a superpower she used to protect her people. Understandably, she was angry with the king for being rewarded with power and riches for his actions, so she cursed his daughter, Aurora.

Khaleesi (*Game of Thrones*) was sold into slavery, abused by her owners, and abandoned by her brother. As the perceived heir to the Iron Throne, she led a campaign to claim the title of Queen and ruler of Westeros. Although her life was plagued by pain and suffering, she was known for her commitment to being a just leader for the realm. Unfortunately, as time went on, the hardship and extreme loss became too much. From her dragon "children" losing their lives in battle to witnessing her handmaiden, advisor, and friend, Missandei, being decapitated by the very people she sought to dethrone, she simply could not catch a break. In the end, instead of freeing the people she swore she would protect, she lost her mind, became the very thing she had been working so hard to dethrone, and burnt the whole city to the ground.

Goob (*Meet the Robinsons*), a boy that lived in an orphanage bedroom with Lewis (the hero of the story), didn't start out as a villain either. Lewis was an inventor who often worked very late into the night, preventing Goob from getting good sleep. When Goob was playing one of his baseball games, he was so tired because of Lewis's late-night routine that he missed the game-winning catch. As time went on, his hatred and enmity toward Lewis grew, resulting in a life full of self-destructive and cruel actions. As an adult, he dedicated himself to ruining Lewis's life and, consequently, the destruction of the world.

At a young age, Zuko (*Avatar: The Last Airbender*), the prince of the Fire Nation, was burned in a fire-bending duel and banished from his own country by his own father. He was told that the only way that he could redeem himself and reclaim his position in his family was to capture and deliver the Avatar, the only person who could stop their conquest, to his father.

Voldemort's (*Harry Potter*) story is a tale of suffering, too. His mother bewitched his muggle (non-magical) father into loving her, even though he would not feel that way about her had he been given the chance. His mother and father eventually split up when the spell wore off on his father; and shortly after Voldemort's birth, his mother died. He was abandoned by his mother in death and his father, who left not realizing she was pregnant, to grow up in an orphanage without love or care.

President Snow's (*The Hunger Games*) mother died in childbirth, too, followed soon after by his father, a military general, who was killed by a rebel sniper. The rest of his life was shaped by these prior events, resulting in more disappointments and frustrations as time passed.

These stories all sing the same song: over time, fear and unprocessed pain can fester and evolve into rage, which then steers villains and influences their choices. And those choices tend to cause suffering for many more people. Like Master Yoda said, "Fear is the path to the dark side. Fear leads to anger. Anger leads to hate. Hate leads to suffering." In fact, we'd like to amend that statement to this: "Fear and pain lead to anger. Anger leads to hate. Hate leads to suffering. And the need to prevent more personal suffering drives villains to instill more fear and suffering in themselves and others." Maybe if these villains had more love or guidance, like Elsa did, they would have had the opportunity to be agents for good.

Of course, pain and suffering are not the be-all and end-all for villain creation. Temptation and intense desires can spark the development of beliefs and actions that result in negative outcomes. Greed, gluttony, jealousy, and especially a lust for power can be the starting point for a life induced by the ever-growing need for *more*. In *The Lord of the Rings*, Saruman is a wizard that became jealous of Gandalf when he was divined the wisest of the wizards by the keeper of the havens, Círdan the Shipwright. He started studying dark magic which led him to become obsessed with the power of the One Ring. He eventually became a servant for Sauron, betraying Gandalf, and helped lead the attempted take-over of Middle Earth.

Which stories include villain back stories and provide you with an opportunity to connect childhood pain to poor choices gone amuck?

How can you share it as an explanation rather than an excuse?

These conversations are crucial to helping children recognize how it's all of the small choices that either develop character or its counterpart. If we can help them to understand what pain will lead to if it's never given expression or empathy or a way to resolve, they will be more likely to address their wounds as they happen and avoid some of those choices that would lead them down a darker path. Of course, it's extremely important that we practice the balance of the explanation of their behavior with the reality that they have had choices along the way and that many of them have obviously been terrible and inexcusable.

Villain Tells

Villains are (usually) clever and deceptive people who usually do their best to hide their true selves and intentions until it's time to reveal themselves and execute their plan. But villains, being imperfect humans, inadvertently drop hints and clues as to who they truly are and what motivates them. Some are more obvious than others, but there are many who successfully hide in the shadows for a long time.

In the *Star Wars* prequel trilogy, Supreme Chancellor Palpatine deceived an entire galaxy into thinking he was working for their benefit, when in fact he was working for his own. Maybe when you watched the movies for the first time, you thought he was working for the "good side." Or maybe you knew he was actually the Sith Lord all along. How did you know that before the movie told you so? Was it his facial expressions? His tone of voice when he talked about certain things? His actions? And if you didn't pick up that he was a villain before the movie disclosed it, when you re-watch the movies, can you pick out specific things that Palpatine did that might suggest he was a villain now that you know that he is one?

These subtle hints and clues are what we call villain tells, and they come in many forms.

The most common way that villains unintentionally expose their actual motives (other than through their actions) is through their facial expressions and tones of voice. If you've watched basically any cartoon, you'll know that villains are often clearly identified purely by how their face or their voice reacts to events that would disgust or horrify a true hero. Sometimes they sneer, stare, or avoid conversation, and other times their voice is deep, dry, and devoid of true emotion.

One of our favorite examples of this is Professor Dolores Umbridge (*Harry Potter*). Her condescending language, her authoritarian tendencies, and her controlling rules clearly revealed her true self; but even before we knew of those traits, we heard her annoying, artificial, high-pitched laugh (not to mention her shit-eating grin). This told us everything we needed to know about this character the moment we met her. As an adult, Michael Goob (*Meet the Robinsons*) wasn't shy about his maniacal laugh, facial expressions, or outward appearance either.

However, not every person that smirks or has a chuckle with a dark tinge is a villain. Professor Severus Snape (*Harry Potter*) is a great example of a character that keeps us guessing. In the beginning of the series, Harry and his friends believed that Professor Snape was helping Voldemort, and therefore a villain, partly due to his reserved expressions and reclusive personality. Plus, there was the strange way he spoke and the deep, dark stares he delivered to our obvious hero and his friends. Even though all of the villain tells might have made us believe that he was indeed a villain, this assessment turned out to be dead wrong. Instead, the reason Professor Snape had a villainous undertone was because he used to act in the interest of one, and later returned to the "good side," where he had to continue the charade of appearing sinister for the good of all. Snape's appearance probably influenced Harry, Ron, and Hermione's initial assumptions about whether or not he was a villain, as it did ours. Isn't it ironic to think about how he turned out to be one of the greatest unsung heroes in the series?

Another way that villains reveal themselves is by projecting their behavior onto others. We think that, sometimes, they do this to convince themselves that they're not the ones behaving badly, in addition to framing or manipulating their enemies. Hans (*Frozen*) convinced Elsa that she was a monster that could not control herself, pushing her to flee her kingdom. Then, he promptly used Elsa's absence as a way to seize control of Arendelle for himself. Scar (*The Lion King*) lied and told Simba that he was responsible for his father's death, when in reality, it was Scar that had murdered him.

And of course, we can't forget the classic villain one-liners. The "Together, we can rule the world," trope is probably one of the most overdone yet brutally honest statements a villain can make. Darth Vader (*Star Wars*) said, "Together, we can rule the galaxy." Councilman Tarrlok (*Legend of Korra*) insisted Korra work with him by joining his task force in order to put an end to the rebellious uprising. Saruman (*The Lord of the Rings*) asked Gandalf to help him aid Sauron's quest to conquer Middle Earth: "We must join with him, Gandalf. We must join with Sauron. It would be wise, my friend." And in *Game of Thrones*, nearly everyone that sought out alliances promised power and riches to those they tried to persuade with little intentions to share any once it was acquired.

These invitations are often paired with the temptation of power because there's always "more power on the dark side." After all, Darth Vader said, "If you only knew the power of the dark side." The way that villains acquire their power, however, always creates weakness. They use deception and raw power that is fueled by pain, anger, and fear, while the greatest heroes are motivated by love, justice, and truth. Take the Lord of the Nazgûl, the Witch-king of Angmar (*The Lord of the Rings*), and Voldemort (*Harry Potter*) for example: They are both empty and frail— mere vessels corrupted by a lust for power and a spirit of rancor. They need and exploit other people's power to survive; and when heroes take their power away, they turn into dust or implode. While the illusion of dark power is tempting, the power and strength of the true hero to rally the forces of good is far greater than the destruction and manipulation of the dark side.

Remember when Anakin Skywalker (*Star Wars*) professed, "Love won't save you, Padme! Only my new powers can do that!" Throughout his whole life, Anakin tried to fix everything, but he couldn't do it all. His mother died, his relationship with his master was waning, and his wife was to meet her demise in childbirth. Thus weakened, he caved to the temptations of the dark side; yet even with all of its "power," he was not able to use it to save anyone he cared about. Instead, he became the very thing he swore to destroy (teehee) and ended up causing more pain and suffering in the process.

Speaking of people becoming the very thing they swear to destroy... it happens a lot, and it's one of the best ways that stories confirm to us that an apparently good character actually has sinister intentions, or that a good person with initially good intentions has crossed the threshold and become a villain. In *Star Wars*, in the middle of a fight with Anakin on the fiery planet Mustafar, Obi-Wan Kenobi tells Anakin, "You have become the very thing you swore to destroy." As a Jedi turned Sith Lord, Anakin had become what he had previously committed his life to defeating. And after insurmountable pain and loss, Khaleesi (*Game of Thrones*) burned down the city that she vowed to protect. Alma Coin, the president of District 13, after she sacrificed Katniss' sister (and so many other children) to win the war, suggested holding a "symbolic" Hunger Games using the children from The Capitol. In other words, the temptation to "make them suffer the same way they made us suffer" was too great a temptation for her to dismiss. Fortunately, Katniss saw what she had become and promptly ended her usurped leadership. Thanks to her, Panem had the opportunity to break their country's cycle of tyranny, barbarity, and injustice.

And perhaps the *most* important villain tell of all is the manner in which the person wields the power given them. We all know that villains want more power for themselves, but what do heroes do with it? While villains try to *take* power away, heroes *refuse* to do so. After the Battle of Hogwarts, Harry (*Harry Potter*) had obtained the Elder Wand, the most powerful wand in the world. When asked what we would do with the wand, he promptly snapped it in half and threw it away. Aragorn, the reluctant king (*The Lord of the Rings*), resisted the power of the ring and accepted his rightful place; but in his first act as king, he bowed to the hobbits. And Neo (*The Matrix*), by being the bridge between man and Machine, brought peace to the Matrix and freed all humans from the unconscious control of the Machines.

> *What were some of the clues that this*
> *person was playing for the dark side?*

> *Ask your children to begin identifying non-*
> *verbals (postures, movements, and expressions)*
> *as well as particular words or behaviors.*

> *Ask. Rewind. Clarify. Validate.*

These are some of the most powerful conversations we have ever had, and they are not just focused on movies and books. Oh no, we have become highly-attuned to villain tells in real-life characters. Imagine the pain our children and our culture could avoid if they could identify darkness when it is so carefully hidden — in themselves and in the world around them.

The Villain Spectrum
The title of Villain is not a label that defines someone as "bad" or "evil." It describes someone who has intentionally and consistently made bad or malicious choices. We often make the mistake of outright calling someone bad as if that's just the way they are, and there's no way to change them, when in fact, there's always a path to redemption.

But we'll talk more about that later.

Life is full of choices, both good and bad, and somewhere in-between. While everyone has certainly made bad choices, villains do not *only* make bad choices. Villains can make a lot of good choices, too, which means that they cannot be completely evil, right? For example, while scheming to take control of the nation, President Alma Coin (*Hunger Games*) showed Katniss an inkling of her remaining humanity when she tried to comfort Katniss after her best friend, Gale, went on a mission to save Peeta. She connected with her about how torturous it is to wait while knowing there's nothing you can do to help a situation, giving us all an insight into how Coin likely felt when her daughter and husband were dying of a disease outbreak years before.

And while some villains are closer to pure evil than others, we would argue that most villains are somewhere between "slightly evil" and "mostly evil." This range of villainary is what we like to call the Villain Spectrum. To understand this spectrum, let's look back at Anakin Skywalker's (*Star Wars*) journey from hero to villain. It started with impulsive revenge and then a decision to kill more in order to save his wife. Think back to the young padawans he killed and the decision to solidify his allegiance with the dark side during his battle with Obi-Wan Kenobi at Mustafar. This series of increasingly disturbing and morally despicable choices are what led Anakin to solidify himself as a villain.

But that's far from the end of Anakin's story.

Surprise your child by asking them,
"What would it take for this villain to become a hero?
Do you think it's possible at this point?"

It's much easier to sort people, ideas, and situations into good or bad, right or wrong, true or untrue, etc. than it is to take the time to observe, discern, be curious, and stay open to being proven wrong about our initial impulse to sort them. Don't get us wrong. Many times, those impulses are right on; but cultivating this level of mindfulness and belief in the human spirit will empower your child. Most importantly, if they don't have to choose between "I'm good" or "I'm a villain" but instead see themselves on a spectrum and know that their attitude and choices can propel them in one direction or the other, they will more quickly bounce back from poor decisions and be more likely to offer those generous assumptions and beliefs to others who appear to be trying to walk away from darker tendencies and paths.

Why Am I So Bad At Being Good?

If there is one thing we've learned through story, it's that the road out of hell is almost always more treacherous than the road to hell. How does someone that has gone down a dark path turn around and choose the light? How do people, and villains in particular, begin to make better choices?

As we discussed in the last section, it all starts with the villain realizing that the choices they have made are wrong. When they begin to see they're creating more problems than solutions, not just for themselves but often for those that they love, they can make better choices. But of course, *making* those choices isn't very easy for the person who has to do it; however, it's never impossible.

In what we have found to be the best redemption arc in television history, Zuko's (*Avatar: The Last Airbender*) personal journey from villain to hero is remarkably deep and has a way of drawing out one's empathy by telling the stories behind his poor decisions. As the son of a tyrannical dictator who wishes to take over the world, one could say that the cards were stacked against Zuko. Guilt and shame were cultivated inside of him at a young age, even to the point where his own father "stripped him of his honor," physically scarred him, and banished him from his country for challenging the decisions made during a war meeting. His father told him that he was not allowed to return until he captured the Avatar, and after nearly three seasons of bad decisions and an unrelenting and uncompromising attempt to restore his honor, he recognized the dire consequences of his actions and made a new choice. He chose to aid the Avatar on his quest rather than capture him. And when he started to make decisions contradicting his past ones, he experienced a crisis of identity, or what Jung would call an ego death. We call it the "transformation flu" at our house.

But it wasn't easy for Zuko to convince the Avatar and friends that he had a change of heart, and understandably so when you consider all of the times that he had tried to thwart their plans and/or kill them. Sparky Sparky Boom Man, anyone? (It's an inside joke. Seriously, go watch the show. Like, right now.) And even when one of the Avatar's friends decided to give him a chance, Zuko accidentally burned her in self-defense when she surprised him in his sleep. His one chance at proving that he had changed seemed like it was gone forever, which prompted him to yell our favorite thing he says in the series: "Why am I so bad at being good?!" This one line beautifully illustrates the challenge of pulling yourself out of the abyss that is a history of bad circumstances and decision-making.

Not too long after that experience, a bounty hunter that Zuko had hired to capture the Avatar attacked their encampment. He confronted him and pleaded with him to stop, but the bounty hunter refused. After he helped the Avatar defeat the bounty hunter, Zuko was reluctantly allowed to join the group. It took a long time for Zuko to earn the trust of everyone he was traveling with, but he did so by consistently righting the wrongs that he, his father, and his country had done to them. In summary, he recognized the consequences of his actions, took responsibility for his misdeeds, and helped heal the people he had hurt by working with them to restore balance to their own lives and the world. That is the path to redemption.

President Business (*The LEGO Movie*), a "control freak" and self-proclaimed perfectionist, saw the world as inherently broken and tried to use glue to make everything "perfect" and "good." Emmet, a not-so-normal construction worker and the creative hero of this story, was eventually able to show President Business that everything can be seen as a creative opportunity to innovate and improve rather than an atrocity to be made into his vision of perfection. Of course, the way Emmet convinced him is a powerful example of the power of looking for the hero in the villain: "You... don't have to be... the bad guy. You are the most talented, most interesting, and most extraordinary person in the universe. And you are capable of amazing things. Because you are the Special. And so am I. And so is everyone. The prophecy is made up, but it's also true. It's about all of us. Right now, it's about you, and you... still... can change everything." As a result of this realization, President Business made the decision to dissolve and destroy the glue that he had imposed on much of the universe, and he even transformed into a better president because of it.

Out of revenge and anger for the King, Maleficent (*Maleficent*) cursed Aurora, the King's daughter, to fall into an eternal sleep at the age of sixteen. But before the curse was able to manifest, Maleficent got to personally know Aurora, and recognized the error of her ways. She even tried to revoke her own curse, but could not do so, dooming Aurora to an everlasting slumber. As the story goes, the curse can only be broken by true love's kiss. In the end, after apologizing for all of her mistakes and swearing to do whatever she could to break the curse, Maleficent kisses Aurora on the forehead and breaks the curse. Because of Aurora, Maleficent learned to love again and was able to see past her pain-filled past and rage-driven ways, and even right her worst wrong.

Anakin Skywalker (*Star Wars*) became a Jedi and started out fighting for the good, but he eventually caved to the dark side and became Darth Vader. He was prophesied to restore balance to the galaxy, which is why many of us viewers were surprised that he turned to the dark side. However, at the last moment, he chose to do the right thing, sacrificed himself for his son, Luke, and destroyed the Sith Lord. In doing so, he redeemed himself and restored balance to'the galaxy albeit not in the way that everyone had imagined.

Although Kenai (*Brother Bear*) wasn't necessarily a villain, he definitely played the role of an antagonist in the beginning of the movie. He was involved in the death of Koda's mother, but as time went on, he was able to walk in the shoes and see through the eyes of his young friend Koda. This awareness allowed Kenai to reflect on his mistakes and prompted him to make it up to Koda by permanently transforming into a bear and committing to be his guardian for a long time to come.

If there's one thing we want you to take away from this chapter, it's that everyone — and we mean *everyone* — is redeemable. All they need is to be given a chance to experience the consequences of their actions and the opportunity to right the wrongs they've inflicted. Think of all of the villains in your life, past and present, and remember that they have good inside of them. When they make a bad choice, we need to call them out on it. But when they make a good one, we can celebrate it. Encourage behavior that reinforces the best of humanity and denounce behavior that's destructive to humanity. Our divine worth is not determined by bad choices that we may make, but by our potential to make better ones.

*Compare and contrast villains.
Explore the similarities and differences and wonder
out loud about why some were able to change
and others were not (or decided not to).*

What was it that opened the door for the shift?

*Separating choice and behavior from worth is the path to
character and freedom. Whenever you are talking about
villains, focus on the word "choices and behaviors,"
rather than using identity/worth language such as
"He is such a bad guy. He was bad from the beginning."*

Carl Jung's wisdom bears repeating here: "We don't get
wounded alone and we don't heal alone." It is true that
many of the initial wounds we all carry were assaults on our
sense of identity and worth. We were "othered" or "abused"
or "mistreated" because someone deemed us unworthy of
love, belonging, or respect. Those identity and worth scars
run deep. They can cause us to do terrible things to avoid
being hurt like that again. And if we perpetuate this idea
that our worth and our behaviors are inseparable, we will
continue to raise generations who lack character and have
no idea how to experience or preserve freedom. But if we
are willing to do the harder work of sitting with each other
in relationships; witnessing wounds and sifting through,
challenging, and renegotiating behaviors, choices, and
wounds; and holding fast to the innate worth and potential
of every human being even in the face of their darkness, we
believe we will soon be enjoying a future with fewer villains
and happier heroes.

Chapter Six

Destiny

"Sometimes the choice isn't
even yours. It's fate."

~ James Cole ~

"**A**aron, we have to finish this. Just a few more episodes, please!" I turned to face him, pleading desperately — not lost to the fact that it seemed our roles had reversed. *Remember the days when he begged me for one more episode or movie when I needed to go to bed?*

He shook his head resignedly. "Mom, I know you are desperate for your answer, but I have school tomorrow. I guess you could finish it by yourself tonight if you have to...?"

"No," I sighed. "You're right. We need to sleep." I kissed him on the cheek and we said goodnight.

But I couldn't sleep. My mind raced. My heart ached. I went to the guest bedroom, so I wouldn't keep hubby awake with my very loud thoughts.

It was early July 2018 and time to write my book, *Upside-Down Messenger.* I'd told the world that it would be out in

September, and my deadline for completing the manuscript was fast-approaching.

But I was stuck. Sit down. Type a few words. Get stuck. Leave the office. Repeat.

What is my problem? It's not like I haven't told this story before, for heaven's sake.

I'd sat in meditation. I'd taken walks. I'd called friends to work through st*ry blocks. Nothing.

Then, Kate had "randomly" called to tell me she was watching *12 Monkeys* and kept feeling like she needed to tell me to check it out. Our history of working through classic books and epic tales together made it impossible for me to ignore her recommendation, even after I looked at the trailer and thought, *Why the hell would I watch this? Time travel? Ugh. Fine, I'll try it.*

Aaron had the same response to the trailer, and I'd begged him to watch it with me on the nights his dad was working. With the smallest of eyerolls, he had agreed.

One episode in, my heart knew the answer was in this story, but my head didn't know what it could be. Two episodes in, my head was spinning — trying to piece together the puzzle that was being offered through various moments in time. One season in, my brain felt like it was melting — struggling to keep track of the characters and timelines, and also stay present so I didn't miss the lesson I knew was coming. Two seasons in, Aaron complained about our pace: "Mom, my brain feels like it's on fire. Why are we watching so many at a time?"

Three seasons in, I was starting to doubt my sanity. *Maybe I'm just crazy. Or maybe this story is making me crazy!*

It was the last season, only (cough) two weeks after we'd started the show (please don't try to count how many episodes and hours we spent daily), and we were just feeling like we had it figured out when the plot twisted on us.

And then my responsible teenager told me it was time to sleep, and I couldn't.

Lying in the soft bed, I stared into the darkness. *What does time travel have to do with my book?* Immediately, I remembered something I'd said to Ursula in an interview just a few months before: "Every time I had an inspiration for the next thing I was going to create, it was as if I time-traveled to the moment of its manifestation in the future; and when I came back to the present moment, I knew it was going to happen and just kept taking the next steps toward that future moment."

My body tingled all over. *It did feel like I was time traveling. Maybe that's part of the answer?*

My mind was finally satisfied enough to let me sleep, and I had plenty of projects to keep it busy the next day while I waited for my story buddy to finish school.

"Okay, Mom. Let's get this answer for you!" He smiled as he plopped onto the couch with his dinner and pressed the PLAY button. His brain may have been melting, but he'd become hooked on this story, too.

We were just a few episodes away from the end when it happened.

One of the gifted heroines was talking to a wounded character who was being hoisted into an ambulance, "You can see time, right? Back to front, like me?"

He nodded.

She continued, "So, let's fast-forward. Skip to the good part. It's all right. Keep going. Just a little bit further. We can do the middle later…"

Energy zipped from the top of my head to my toes. "That was it!" I exclaimed, reaching over to hit pause. "Aaron, that's what I did!"

He smiled, obviously relieved, even though he didn't completely understand.

When we finished the show, I kissed him goodnight and then sat in the dark room, my mind swirling and processing. I have no idea how long I was sitting there, but I'm pretty sure I traveled between my pasts and futures for at least an hour before I was too tired to think or sit up anymore.

The next morning, Aaron sat across from me at the table with his coffee and said, "So, tell me about this answer."

I took a deep breath, wondering where to start. "Well, this whole show was about the attempt to break Time, right?"

He nodded affirmatively.

"And why did they want to break It?" I asked.

"Maybe… to forget all the pain… They seemed to hate this world…" He searched for an answer while he responded.

"Right. Think about Olivia and all of the pain, betrayal, and disappointment she endured since her childhood. If you thought you could break Time and it would allow you to forget the past, wouldn't that goal make sense?"

One eyebrow raised, he turned the tables on me. "So, how is this an answer for *you*?"

"Well, I think I was a Time Traveler," I said with a smirk.

He shook his head in that "Mom, you're so drama" kinda way.

"No, really. When I was initially inspired with that series of books, it was like stepping into an alternate timeline with a whole future that was waiting for me to wake up to it. I didn't sit around and conjure a bunch of possibilities — they were given to me. I saw the future as if it was already there... as if I was already there — the series of books, the teacher from *The Secret*, the bestseller list, and the training company."

He nodded, as if he'd heard me tell the story a million times (cuz he had), and was ready for the new part. Then, his eyes widened with awareness. "Mom, that's kinda how I felt when I got the invitation to go to Australia, remember? It was like I read the paperwork and *I just knew I was supposed to be on that trip.* And you were trying to help me hold reasonable expectations for the process, but I knew I was already as good as there."

"Exactly! The difference is that you were eleven years old and had fewer limiting beliefs and failures stacked up against you. For me, when the inspiration hit, I was a hot mess in every area of my life. But somehow, I left that broken, lost, hopeless version of me and stepped into another version of myself — one that felt more true... and powerful... and whole..." I paused, savoring the feeling of the memory. "I don't know how, but I hit fast-forward... skipped to the good part... attracted the resources I needed."

His eyes sparkled a bit as the pieces started to lock together. "Just like how all the resources for the Australia trip came together as I tried one thing after another to raise money."

"Right. But because I had limiting beliefs and wounds to face, I had to do about three years of 'coming back to do the middle' while I figured out how to get from my head into my heart to facilitate transformation for others."

He took another sip, waiting for me to continue.

"But after I did some of that middle work, I fast-forwarded again. For three years, I unearthed, honed, leveraged, and expanded my superpowers. I grew a business really quickly and organically. I hit bumps in the road, learned lessons, and came out the other end even stronger. I became a trusted guide and collected allies. I had somehow fast-forwarded to the best version of myself I'd ever met. She was a courageous badass who time-traveled to future moments, created insane goals, and somehow achieved them. She was seen, heard, appreciated, and loved. She was the ME I had known was locked away inside of me for a long time. She was my Destiny. I saw and stepped into the truer me, the business expansion, the two-hundred-person events, and even wrote my own book in just a few weeks..."

"And then the time travel stopped..." he said, as if reading my mind.

"Yes, because I had to come back and 'do the middle'..."

"And your middle looked a bit like his, eh?" he asked, gulping the cooling liquid.

"Yes, I mean, I wasn't physically on the verge of death; but one of the wounds I'd been carrying from my past had been demanding attention for two years, and the stakes were getting too high. It hit me relationally with my colleagues, financially in the business, and eventually physically when that guy attacked me. I had to figure out what was causing this mess."

Wow, you really can't make this sh*t up, I thought as I realized how perfectly destined it all seemed — all the way down to the timing of me launching this second book, my friend finding and recommending this show, and the other show we had been watching as a family.

"Aaron, you know that Bible series we've been watching? Peterson's?"

"Oh yeah," he nodded.

"Well, he just finished helping us consider the Genesis stories from a psychological perspective. Think about what he said about Cain — that he felt all of Life was unfair and came to resent It to the point where he would kill his own brother, who was receiving nothing but blessings for his efforts."

"Oooooh... like the people who wanted to break Time..." He glanced out the window, obviously processing some of these new connections.

"Right, and then the next book of the Bible is Exodus, and I cannot wait for him to do a series on that. The Israelites — the children of God — were destined for life in the Promised Land but living as slaves in Egypt. Moses was found and raised by the Pharaoh's daughter and then called to help his people escape their masters. You've heard about the parting of the Red Sea?"

He nodded.

"Okay, so think about that. They were destined for the Promised Land — the land of flowing milk and honey — and God delivered them. But then, they walked around in circles for forty years before getting there. A whole generation died before they could enter."

"Why?" he asked.

"Well, I was always told it was because they were disobedient, but now I'm thinking the wilderness was their 'middle.'"

He cocked his head, his lack of familiarity with the story impacting his ability to make all of these connections with me.

"If you're destined to be a free child of God, but you're raised in slavery, you don't know anything other than taking orders and being fed and sheltered in exchange for your service. So, maybe the Israelites were doing the tough 'middle work' of discovering and releasing all of the ways they were still enslaved in their minds. *They had to learn how to be free.* They had to learn the rules of life from the very beginning — how to take care of (and eventually defend) themselves and each other, how to trust God's word above appearances, and how to raise free children who would fulfill their destiny."

"Hmmmm..."

"So, back to me. I time travel to the future and meet my Destiny for a while, but you know where I came from. While that powerful part of me was creating magic, there was another part that was completely enslaved to all of the old st*ries (or Fate) of needing those people to take care of me rather than relying on my real Source... of trying to prevent and fix the messes around me that weren't mine rather than let those people face their consequences... of taking care of everyone else's big feelings but never feeling or processing my own. Aaron, this is my *middle*. I had to come back and face the wounds and heal the st*ries, so that I can actually live my

Destiny, rather than vacillate between magical moments of Destiny and crushing moments of Fate."

"And you're going to write about this in your book?" he asked, looking for that last connection.

"No. Well... maybe? But I think the reason I haven't been able to write is because I haven't wanted to go back. The moments I'm going to write about are just so magical that it hurts to remember them and then come back to life in 'the middle.' This season is hard — staring these old st*ries in the face and having to write new ones without a model..." I said, a tear slipping down my cheek. "But you know what? I wouldn't change it. I wouldn't go back to any part of my life and make a different choice... because every choice I made led me here and I like the person I'm becoming and the life that is emerging for me... and us..."

"Sounds like the show we just finished," he said with a smirk as he stood up from the kitchen table and took a few steps to kiss my forehead before reciting the words of one of the characters: "'There are many endings, but the right one is the one you choose.'"

Destiny, Fate, and Time

What did you learn about Destiny, Fate, and Time, from your favorite childhood stories? Did you learn that there is one way the story will end (fate) if the hero doesn't make the choices necessary to change the story's trajectory and fulfill their destiny? What did you learn about the importance of the hero's destiny to the rest of their family, their community, and their world? And how did you feel about Time? Did you learn that it was something to begrudge, race against, and fight, or something to slow down, savor, and even trust?

Looking back at my earliest childhood stories, I see stories of heroes like Maverick (*Top Gun*) and Doug (*Iron Eagle*), who seem to have been born with the exact-right combination of strengths and ambitions to do what they were called to do, but who also spent long hours in preparation, honing their natural abilities. Whether the calling was external or internal and whether they believed they were meant to do it or not, effort and training were required, and so were the wounds. The wounds and fears of more loss and pain somehow compelled them and focused their efforts. (These heroes also validated my inner rebel who innately knew that I would eventually have to get over my desire to fit in and face the fact that who I am and what I am here to do requires me to take big risks and make others feel uncomfortable and even scared in the process.) I marveled at how it seemed like all of the mentors and resources seemed perfectly placed and timed. I mean, it's a freaking miracle that the talented young pilot's friends were already primed with the knowledge and access required to steal two jets and save his father (*Iron Eagle*).

Then there was the element of Faith in one's call of Destiny and in oneself. When Ray (*Field of Dreams*) heard the words, "Build it and they will come," he had a choice. He was either going to call it a lapse in judgment, or he was going to dig his heels in and do the work required to manifest the miracle. It took longer than he'd hoped, but who wouldn't feel impatient with that miracle on its way?

Of course, when it came to Time, Peter Pan and Hook gave me a pretty clear picture of the chaos that emerges when Time is too important, or not important enough. It matters, but it shouldn't control us. Maybe most importantly, Bastian (*Neverending Story*) inspired the possibility that we are all deeply connected, through books and stories and even timelines and that our choice to believe that we are part of the bigger story and to behave as if that's true can change everything for everyone connected to us by any means.

Now that you have identified some of the patterns in your early exposure to Destiny, Fate, and Time (and maybe Faith, too!), how have those ideas affected the way that you see and relate to yourself, your potential, and your purpose? Are you compelled to fulfill your Destiny, or fight your Fate, and what would happen if you just followed the script that has already been written for you by your genetics and your culture? Can you see how even your wounds may be part of your bigger heroic story? Do you naturally expect resources to show up to help you, and do you expect them to come at exactly the last moment possible? And do they? Do you notice evidence that who you are and the choices you are making to fulfill your Destiny are positively impacting everyone around you?

These lessons about Destiny, Fate, Time, and I would add Faith, have deeply impacted the way I see myself and behave in the world. The moment I sat down to outline my book series and saw how all of my desires could be fulfilled because of the painful childhood wounds and the many plot twists in my career path, it felt like I had found my Destiny. That feeling expanded when I met *The Secret* teacher a few months later and every time I have looked up over the last fifteen years and realized that all of the resources I needed to answer the next call of Destiny were right there waiting for me. And, when life wasn't feeling deliciously destined, there was always another story to remind me that there is a Timing to Destiny that we cannot push or pull, but maybe there is some room for negotiation...

There is no way William Parrish (*Meet Joe Black*) can avoid Death when he walks into his life, but he does negotiate a little delay of his inevitable end.

In *Life is Beautiful,* Guido can't change the fact that he and his son are separated from the woman they love, or what will eventually happen to them at the camp, but his choice to activate his son's imagination and make a game out of life at the concentration camp protected his son's mind and heart from the atrocities of war.

When Evan's attempts to "right the past" (*The Butterfly Effect*) ended up altering his present dramatically in completely unexpected ways, it made me rethink my dreams of going back in time and doing something differently.

Joe's journey of opening up to the possibility that his wife was trying to communicate with him in *The Dragonfly* reminded me of the importance of following all of the signs that are leading us to our destiny.

The Matrix was one of those experiences that really made me wonder how much control The Architect and The Oracle have, and whether they knew their plan would be revised by The One all along or if they could do anything about it.

I laughed out loud while watching *The Adjustment Bureau,* mostly because it was easy for me to imagine that all of my diversions from my pre-written plan were probably making my supernatural team slap their foreheads and work overtime. The idea that there was a pre-written fate for David that leveraged all of his strengths and pain for the common good was a good reminder, and so was the idea that his insistence on also experiencing Love would disrupt the Plan until the MapMaker realized he was serious.

Groundhog Day was one of those incredible reminders that we get caught in painful st*ry or fate loops until we find that one new script or behavior that changes the trajectory of the entire story and leads us to a better destiny. And newsflash, it always comes back to choosing Love.

And of course, *About Time's* time-traveling Tim demonstrates that if we had the opportunity to go back to change or control situations, we would eventually learn that it's a lot easier and more honoring of others to be in the present moment and savor it.

I Couldn't Have Made This Up

It was that wonderful time once again. Eleven-year-old me sitting on the couch with my mom, facing the towering 60-something inch flat screen in my great grandmother's living room, and watching none other than one of the greatest series ever (for probably the hundredth time): *Harry Potter.*

This event occurs *at least* twice per year, and usually when I'm sick. I swear, *Harry Potter* is infinitely magical and by far the best medicine. By the time I finish watching all of the movies back-to-back, my sickness is gone — poof! But this time, I wasn't sick. I just needed some more magic in my life.

In the middle of the movie, my mom, as she often does, paused the freakin' movie. As you can imagine, I rolled my eyes and let out an audibly irritated sigh.

"Yeah, yeah, I know," she said as I turned around to meet her eyes. She was doing that thing again where she asked me a hard question about what we were watching. *Ugh.* "I have to know, who's your favorite character?"

When I shot back, "Professor McGonagall!" my mom was visibly stunned, obviously not expecting that answer.

"Wow, that's not who I would have guessed. What do you like about her?"

Well, she's a great character, of course. Head of Gryffindor house, very supportive, talented, fearless, boundlessly dedicated to her students, and of course, you can't forget that epic and hilarious scene in The Deathly Hallows Part 2 when she enchanted the Hogwarts suits of armor to defend the castle during the Battle of Hogwarts. I still giggle every time I hear her gleefully say, "I've always wanted to use that spell!" in the middle of a war zone.

Sorry, got a little carried away there.

Okay, so she's a great person and kinda funny sometimes. So what? How does that make her my favorite character?

Well, this is what I had to say at the time.

"She is really awesome. She's powerful and kind. She always assumes they are trying to do the right thing, even when they are actually breaking the rules."

"Ah… yes. She is really fair and helpful." My mom stared at me blankly for a second before she picked up the remote, resumed the movie, and walked out of the room to grab a snack.

Fast-forward a few months to me coming home from school. I had opened the front door and plopped my backpack down with less care than usual. My best friend had just turned eleven, and I was upset. The aggressive thwomp caught my mom's attention.

"Hey, Buddy. How was your day?" she asked in her trademark chipper and genuinely inquisitive tone. (It's a miracle she still asks me even after all of the times I simply say "*It was good.*") I shifted my gaze to hers and squeezed out a half-hearted smile.

"It was okay…" I was unconvincing to say the least.

"Are *you* okay?" Concerned with my apparent upset, she put her hand on my arm as she pulled out of the school's parking lot.

"Well…" I pursed my lips together. "My friend just turned eleven, and he didn't get his invitation to Hogwarts."

Her eyebrows shot up. "Oh." This was the kind of caught-off-guard "oh" that people say when they realize their ten, nearly-eleven-year-old still believes Hogwarts is real and that he would be receiving his invitation when he turned twelve. "I'm so sorry, buddy. That sucks."

There was a long pause before she asked, "If you were to get your invitation to Hogwarts, would you go? Would you leave your friend?"

"Mom, I would leave *you* to go to Hogwarts." There was even less hesitation than when she had asked me who my favorite character was. Her face went from inquisitive, to surprised, to understanding as she thought more about my answer.

"You know, if you really felt like that was where you were meant to be and found your people and mentors, I would want you to go, too… even if it was hard."

And that's when she put it all together: The reason that my favorite character was Professor McGonagall, and my deep desire to go to Hogwarts myself, was because I needed some "magic" in my education and special teachers to help me unlock my potential—just like Professor McGonagall.

And as we all know from Chapter 3, finding mentors and seeking proper training seems to become a deep desire as one begins to "cross the threshold" from simply living to stepping into the greater quest that one is meant to embark upon.

Flash-forward *again*. We're living in Oregon over one year later and I'm walking into my first Mock Trial class at my new "school" called Village Home. I had heard great things about the instructor of the class from my first year, but I didn't have a class with her until my second year.

You already know from previous chapters how much I loved Mock Trial, but a big part of that love is thanks to Teacher Deborah, my very own Professor McGonagall. As I got to know her more, I found that there were many distinct similarities in her teaching style to that of Professor McGonagall. I know that sounds crazy, but I kid you not... How much she reminded me of the professor was one of the first things I thought of during that first class. And later, I found out that she ran a *Harry Potter*-themed class as "Professor Deborah" and had referred to herself a couple times as Professor McGonagall.

You can't make it up, man.

That's not to say she was the only "professor" that came into my life at the right time—there were many others, including my ethics and literature instructor, my science instructor, the school paper's instructor, and of course, my improv instructor who decided to leave Village Home right after I graduated.

Just as Harry with Dumbledore (*Harry Potter*) and Luke with Obi-Wan Kenobi (*Star Wars*), my mentors appeared at just the right time; and after I learned exactly what I needed, they disappeared.

But, let's rewind for a quick minute, since we're talking here about Destiny. One of the first classes I took at Village Home was called The Human Spark. It focused on Human Evolution and capabilities. From a scientific perspective, what makes humans human? It's strange to think about now, but this class opened up a whole can of... well... potential... within me regarding what it means to be human and what human potential is.

Around two months into the first term, I got an email from my aunt, Alyssa, asking me if I would be willing to review a college paper of hers titled "Harnessing Human Potential." It was *interesting* timing to say the least, especially when you consider she sent me the email not twenty minutes after my Human Spark class that day.

I agreed, and instead of doing my class work, I spent two hours in the library digging straight into that paper, looking for insight and asking questions. When I sent my feedback along with a few hard questions to Alyssa, I'm pretty sure her exact words were, "I wasn't expecting a whole ass dissertation."

I guess you could say her paper *sparked* something in me… in more ways than one.

Not even a week later, I began work on a work sample for The Human Spark class. Because I wanted to stay out of the standard education system matrix, I joined a proficiency-based charter school program that required me to provide work samples for every class I took to show what I was learning and how I was applying that knowledge. I mostly wrote short essays for my work samples, and this time was no exception. I called it "What Makes Us Human" and took the reader on an evolutionary journey by exploring the connections between human potential and our physical manifestation(s), and wrapping it all up with something a little more… abstract. Just read the ending paragraph for yourself:

"We are imaginative, ingenious, and creative beings filled with potential. I don't know if we need science to tell us that the human spark lives within us all, and that it is up to us to harness that potential within ourselves, to lift each other out of darkness, uncertainty, and chaos, to a brighter and enlightened future. That's the human spark."

For the next month or so after that, a tsunami of creative inspiration, insight, and ideas flooded my waking and resting hours led me to roughly outline an entire fantasy book series. Its purpose—to explore what it means to live in the unknown, conquer chaos, and harness the human spark from the perspective of the protagonist *and* the antagonist. Unfortunately, it's almost two years later and it's still just an outline. But after all of those "coincidences," I'm certain that pausing work on the project will turn out to be the best thing that could've happened for both it and me.

Oh yeah, and when I started planning out this chapter—the last one to be written—I realized that each of the themes in this book (Uncertainty, Self-Knowledge, Destiny, etc.) directly correlate with the major phases of my book series... What the hell?!

I know The Matrix series has trained us to be suspicious, or even scared of dejá vu, but damn it if I'm not a sucker for synchronicities.

At this point, I wouldn't blame you for thinking that I'm crazy for believing all of these things weren't coincidences at all, and instead some kind of "destiny." A few years ago, I would have agreed with you. But I have to tell you, in hindsight, it's difficult for me to brush off all of the opportunities and people that have appeared for me exactly when I needed them.

For example, when I decided to go down a non-traditional educational path, a network full of insightful change-makers and mentors appeared. They helped me figure out what I like to do and don't like to do according to my innate wiring and personality which helped me to hone in on some possible career paths. From there, I got the inspiration to start a business, Caterbuilder (pronounced like caterpillar), that helps entrepreneurs and small businesses build their next dream from the ground up. And when I say I got the "inspiration," what I mean is that every single step from its inception all the way to its creation let me know that it was the right next thing for me to do: The workshop that was offered to me from a wonderful family friend, the way that the brand lined up with the butterfly metaphor that my mom weaved into her life and business, and the logo that not only looks like a caterpillar but also matches the flow of my signature since I learned how to write in cursive.

It took about nine months of experimenting with and searching for the work I love the most when I realized that I was happiest when the work I do is novel to me, involves lots of checklists, smart systems, and incredible teams of people. I became determined to find out how I could do and experience more of those things, and instead of finding the answer, the answer found me: project management. And what do you know? A month later, a huge pilot project for the state of New Mexico showed up and needed my help with the guidance of an incredible mentor (who also showed up at the most perfect time imaginable). Don't even get me started on the project management certification course that landed at my feet barely one month into the project—it's so exciting to me!

Yes, I do realize that's the nerdiest thing ever.

Regardless of what anyone thinks, I can't help but feel like I've been prepared with just the right experiences at just the right times so I can grow and do the next big thing; and

I'm not the only one who feels that way. I would be remiss if I didn't tell you about how, right after I started my business, my mom had received a lot of signals (And, I mean, *a lot*. She couldn't get them to shut up, actually!) that told her to transform her business from a one-woman show into a team venture. And I'm proud to say I'm one of her "elves" in our ever-evolving and growing "Toy Factory."

Oh, and did I forget to mention that she brought together 19 authors, including me, to write a book about this exact subject? In *You Can't Make This St*ry Up: What If It's All Happening for Us?*, I and several of my mom's friends, colleagues, and past-and-current clients wrote about how we've healed our stories and experienced what can only be described as divine synchronicities through the writing process. In my chapter, I talk more about the story with my great-grandmother (the same one that I wrote about in Chapter 5: Redemption) and how my last experience with her, although bittersweet, came at the exact right time and prepared me for her passing.

So yeah, I believe in destiny, and if you don't already, then I invite you to adopt a different perspective… just as a little experiment. Consider that everything that happens "to" you—the good, the bad, and the really ugly—is actually happening *for* you and preparing you for a greater purpose. As we know from *Harry Potter*, *The Matrix*, *The Lord of the Rings*, and even *The* (freaking) *Lego Movie*, surrendering to prophecy unlocks free will, removes resistance, and leads you to better possibilities than you could ever imagine.

The moment we realize that we have the power to choose Destiny over Fate is absolutely intoxicating. Mesmerized by "what could be" and determined to replace the "what is," we start taking action. And for a few moments, that deep knowing that we are meant for more compels us and appears to be affirmed at every turn. How could we not have seen this our whole life, right? And then, something happens. We realize that Fate still has its claws in us and that it's going to take a little more effort than we imagined to end its reign in our lives.

If we're honest, we immediately wonder if it's possible to go back out the way we came in. In contrast to the vision of who we are meant to be, we see the parts of us that are not aligned with The Magical End we know is possible. It's grueling and sometimes lonely work to engage and cultivate love for the parts of us that are wounded and don't believe in our Destiny — even when we know our allies are at the mouth of the cave, keeping watch (*Korra*) and praying for us.

If we stick to it, we get to drop all of the heavy dreams, expectations, and masks of both Fate and Destiny. We find out what we're really made of, who we really are, and why we're really here. We realize that our Destiny is ours alone — that it's not a static map that we have to follow or fit into, but a masterful collaboration and negotiation between us and The One who made the first map. And, most importantly, we realize that Love is the WHY and the HOW of unfolding it.

Eventually, we recognize that we never really left The Magic (or The Magic never really left us) because our Co-Author will continue to connect with us in the most remarkable ways — even when we're sitting on our couch, with our kid, wondering why we can't write a book. Maybe Destiny is right here, right now, and we just don't need to worry so much.

Diving Deeper into Destiny
with Your Kids and Their Stories

Your Destiny Wants You

In a culture that is largely focused on the material world and consumption, it is easy to feel like this meaning and Destiny conversation is complicated and challenging. But we believe it's quite the opposite; we believe that our Destiny wants us so hard (as Aaron says) that it is constantly sending us clues and opportunities to discover, pursue, and live it.

And all of the greatest stories seem to support this idea of prophecies and destinies being fulfilled, and heroes being led to each important moment of decision about them. Orphaned boys like Luke Skywalker and Harry Potter were hidden from the world until it was time for them to begin their training. At just the right moments, their mentors appeared and invited them to learn who they really were and were always meant to be. Neo was told to follow the white rabbit, offered the red pill, and then inspired by riddles from the Oracle on his path to realizing that he was The One. Even James Cole (*12 Monkeys*) seemed to be guided back and forth through time through surprising clues to save the world and eventually realize that he would have to sacrifice himself to do it.

Our Destiny wants us, and It seems to pull us, nudge us, drive us, and inspire us to the next experience we need in order to discover and live it. What if It is determined to do the same with you and your child?

Which stories and characters give you the opportunity to explore Destiny? Which journeys will help you begin revealing heroes' intersections of natural talents,

experiences, training, and opportunities —
and the moments of their Destiny realized?

Wonder out loud about the relevant connections to any
intersections you are witnessing for your child, and ask
them how they feel about all that. And then respect their
response. They might not be able to see any of this for
now, but your question will nonetheless plant a seed.

Isn't it amazing that you get to witness your child discover
their Destiny? What might happen if we let go of all of
our assumptions about what will make our child's future
healthier and happier, and just joined in on the quest
of uncovering who they are and why they are here? We
truly believe this is one of the main reasons we have had
zero power struggles in our relationship. We are partners
and allies on this journey of unfolding Destiny, and it is
so much fun.

Your Fate is In Your Hands
Fate, in our estimation, is the probable future in the absence
of awareness, free will, action, and perseverance. No matter
our background, we all come into this world with our own
set of identities, circumstances, and people. Some of us
are dealt some extremely challenging and even devastating
combinations of these; others somehow escape severity but
find themselves facing their own set of challenges. Katniss's
fate (*Hunger Games*) appeared to be sealed at The Reaping
for her district, when she chose to interrupt Fate's hand and
take her sister's place in the games; and yet it wasn't. She
figured out how to play the hand that was dealt to her in a
way that would force the hand of the villain. James Cole's
fate (*12 Monkeys*) appeared to be sacrificing himself until
a doctor and Time conspired for another ending. Whatever
the level of suffering we enter into or find ourselves in,

there's always the possibility that it could form the forever story of our life — become our fate — if we let it.

> *What are the stories that portray the potentials of Destiny and Fate? Which characters look to be fated to an unhappily ever after, or set up perfectly for success? What actually happens?*

> *Play a game with your child to explore these concepts and see what happens. Ask them to convince you with story (and even personal) examples that Fate is impossible to change.*

> *Then, ask them to convince you with story (and even personal) examples that a person's choices can change their Fate. Then ask them what feels truer and more empowering.*

Wouldn't it be amazing if it was easy and fun and fruitful to play devil's advocate with your child — if it was so natural that it was a rare occasion for them to feel like you were just giving them a hard time or trying to convince them of something you believe? We started this process long ago with Story — challenging each other's assumptions, wondering out loud about each other's conclusions, etc. And we love it. It isn't always easy to look at the stuff that we point out; but the process and outcome is always worth the discomfort. Learning how to debate both sides of the same issue expands our perspective and our empathy and our ability to sort through information and situations from multiple perspectives and come to much more balanced conclusions. This "possibility thinking," we believe, is what empowers every child to move beyond the script that Fate has given them and choose their Destiny.

Time is An Illusion
When we're young, our sense of Time is one way; as we grow older, it's another. What's the difference? Responsibilities and obligatory tasks to be crammed into

a day? When we feel like we are stuck in a Fate loop, our sense of Time is different than when we feel like we are pursuing or living our Destiny. Time doesn't change. Our perception of it does.

But when it comes to the conversation of Destiny, the concept of Time plays an extremely important role. There were two big moments of awareness around this for us, which started with a True to Intention client and ended with a True To Intention lesson.

First, the concept of Time ending — or Death — is clarifying. In 2012, a client called and requested help immediately to complete his book because his doctors had given him only thirty days to live. Knowing his time was almost up, his top three values and goals became extremely clear: 1) Integrity — He had to deliver on his promise to marry his wife in a church, 2) Legacy — He had to finish his book and make sure that everything he had learned didn't leave with him, and 3) Family — He had to make sure that his personal and professional family details were in order. Since taking this incredible ride with him, the question "What would I say and do if I knew I only had 30 days left?" is one that regularly brings clarity when we feel we have lost our way the way that Tim's (*About Time*) father's mortality changed his desire to be anywhere else but the present moment and to do it so well that he wouldn't feel the need to go back and do it again.

Years later, around the time we were mind-melting with *12 Monkeys,* we were talking about how conflicting it was to feel personally stuck and frustrated while watching others around us succeed. Why weren't we arriving at our Destinations? It was a beautiful spring day in Oregon when the answer came after a stomp around the neighborhood and questions (more like demands of) the Co-Author, "Why...? How...? When...?" The answers came at the moment of noticing that of the hundreds of trees on the walk, only the pink blossoms were budding. The red ones would come next and eventually the white ones would emerge. We'd marveled at this apparently predetermined blossom script in nature for two years in the Pacific Northwest, but that day, it was a message: "Maybe we are the white-blossomed tree and our friends are the pink ones. Maybe we're not doing anything wrong; maybe it's just not our time according to The Schedule." Something about that possibility shifted our entire perspective around Time. The invitation was to stop trying to change and control Time and the events happening in it (like the character in our favorite stories) and to simply savor whatever phase or moment we are in and do what we can in the moment to make it even better.

Even at the cultural level, this seems to be a more powerful way to approach change and Time. Eugenia (*The Help*) was determined to change the way a whole group of people were seen and treated; and while she wished she could change the hearts and minds and her entire culture overnight, the reality was that it was going to have to take however long it took for enough individuals to object to the status quo and change it. Even when something *should* change overnight as a moral imperative, we have to learn to deal with the real factor of Time.

In every story we've ever engaged that has Time as one of its major themes, the message has always been the same: "Humans are clearly extremely powerful co-creators, but Time is not one of those things they can control or change without serious consequences."

What are some of the time-themed stories you could use to spark this conversation? Which characters' journeys will create opportunities to talk about seasons and cycles of growth, and explore how our perspective of Time can change our experience of it?

Wouldn't it be amazing if children could hold fast to those childhood tendencies when it comes to Time — to imagine that it will never end and to get lost in it? What might happen if we taught them about the seasons of life and nature and empowered them to unsubscribe from some of the modern beliefs that we should achieve certain milestones on other people's timelines? What if the stories we engage could help us have a more balanced view of ourselves inside this crazy illusion we call Time — to see ourselves not as Its victims, but as Its stewards? We say let's at least give this a worthy attempt and see if we can raise a generation more in tune with and at ease with themselves and with Life and where It's taking them.

Chapter Seven
Leadership

"For years and years, I chased their cheers. The crazy speed of always needing more. But when I stop and see you here, I remember who all this was for. And from now on, these eyes will not be blinded by the light."

~ P.T. Barnum ~

"**I**s everyone out? Is everyone okay?" a panicked Phineas T. Barnum (*The Greatest Showman*) asked Phillip Carlyle as the circus building burned down and people ran away from it.

"Yeah, yeah," Phillip answered.

Realizing that the woman he loved was still in the building, Phillip went back into the flames to find her. Phineas followed his friend right before the woman appeared from another direction.

Aaron and I held our breath with his family and the town members who watched parts of the building collapse and the fire roar. And, in ridiculous mommy messenger style, I paused it.

"Mom!" Aaron exclaimed, sitting up and looking at me indignantly.

"I know. I know. But look at this, Aaron." I waved my hand to the image of the circus on fire. "What happened? How did this man go from having the love and respect of his family, partner, and employees to having his entire life and work burning down?"

"I don't know, Mom. You're killing me. I want to see how this ends." He flopped back into the couch, exasperated with me.

"Okay, let's see how it ends, but I really want us to think about this before we walk away from this screen tonight. It's so important." I clicked the PLAY button and we breathed a sigh of relief as Phineas emerged with Phillip on his shoulders. My attention, however, was only half-there as my mind drifted back through the previous scenes of the movie to find the moment that Phineas had lost his way.

I'm so tired of watching truly gifted, inspired, and powerful visionaries and entrepreneurs lose their way. I feel like I'm a short step away from it myself every day.

A few minutes later, tears poured down my cheeks when those he'd abandoned confronted him and asked him to "come home."

"Okay," I said as I wiped my face and clicked off the tv. "Where did he go wrong?" I had some ideas, but I knew our conversation would help me the rest of the way there.

Aaron had obviously been thinking about it, too. "Well, he stopped listening to his partner and went really big even though he was warned it would be a bad idea."

"Yes, he was a risk-taker but that had consistently worked *for* him up to a certain point. What had changed for him this time around?"

"He stopped listening to the people who loved him. His wife tried to talk to him and Carlyle did, and he ignored both of them."

"Good point. Did anything happen before that to make him feel it was okay to dismiss people who loved him?"

He paused for a minute, searching the scenes in his head. "Well, I didn't like how he pushed his friends out of the party." He paused again, reflecting more deeply. "It was that singer lady. Something went horribly wrong when she arrived in the story..." He kept searching. "Yeah, I think he changed the first time he watched her sing. Something happened," he surmised, still not sure what it was.

But clarity had just struck me at my core. "What were the words in the song, Aaron?"

"Never enough..." he started to sing it and then his eyes widened as all of the dots began to connect.

"Exactly! Think about his childhood and how he felt about his father and how he was mistreated by her father. He always felt 'never enough,' and that idea actually helped him become really resourceful and surround himself with people who could help him make his circus dream real. But you're right. Something happened when she sang." I paused, trying to remember the details. "Remember how, right after he introduced her to his in-laws, his father-in-law said something to him? What was it?"

I picked up the remote and went back to the scene. We both leaned forward as we watched Phineas try to make the point that his father-in-law had been wrong about him, only to hear him say, "All that fortune, and still just the tailor's boy."

Quickly, the singer raised a glass and toasted him publicly with more-than-affirming words, "To Mr. Barnum, who has shown once and for all that a man's station is limited only by his imagination." And then privately shared, "I sometimes feel like I don't belong here. I was born out of wedlock and that brought shame upon my family. And life always manages to remind me that I don't deserve a place in this world, and that leaves a hole that no ovation can ever fill."

This time, Aaron paused it. "Never enough. Nothing will ever be enough to fill that hole. And that's how he had felt his whole life." I nodded and he continued, "And right after that is when he pushed his friends out of the party and started making very selfish decisions to *get more.* His wife asked him when it would ever be enough, and he still kept going." His clear eyes sparkled with clarity.

"That's why the last few words of the movie are so important, 'It's everything you ever want. It's everything you ever need. And it's here right in front of you...'" We sat in silence as the full weight of this hit both of us. "This is a very important awareness, Aaron. I face it in my industry and have actually recoiled at becoming a leader because I know that I have similar wounds of feeling like I have had to prove my value to everyone all the time. And I've watched so many of my colleagues listen to people who consciously or unconsciously prey on those old 'never enough' wounds. They acknowledge the gift like she did and then promise success, worthiness, and *more*. But then they always end up leading them to make selfish decisions *to achieve more,* that actually hurt the people around them, including the people who helped them reach their first level of success. I only know of a few who have avoided this fate."

Leadership

In your favorite childhood stories, how was leadership defined and depicted? What were the qualities of the leaders you esteemed, and what were the pitfalls of the "bad leaders"? What did you think about the leaders who ruled over empires (think Disney's kings and queens) and the revolutionaries who overthrew them (*Robinhood*)? Were there any leaders of households, classrooms, and boardrooms in your favorite stories; or was your conversation around leadership confined to territories and subjects?

When I look at the leaders I watched in my childhood, I see leaders who were destined for the throne (*Sword in The Stone*) and those who rose to their status and position because they earned the trust and respect of people who believed in their vision, their capacity to accomplish what they set out to achieve (*Field of Dreams*), and their willingness to sacrifice their own desires and comforts for the sake of others (Jesus of Nazareth and King Arthur). In contrast, there were leaders who were either evil to begin with or corrupted by the amount of power they acquired (*Man in The Iron Mask*), those who deceived their followers (*Wizard of Oz*), and those who wielded their positions with heavy-hands (*Footloose* and *Dirty Dancing*), a good dose of human frailty cloaked by hypocrisy (*Thorn Birds*), and a whole lot of self-preservation and/or self-absorption (*The Little Mermaid* and oh-so-many Soap Opera family patriarchs/monarchs and executives).

Now that you have identified some of the patterns in your early exposure to leadership, how have those ideas about leaders, and leadership itself, informed your experience in the world as a parent, a citizen and community-member, and/or as an entrepreneur or change agent? Have they made you more trusting, or wary, of leaders? Did they inspire you to become a leader or to avoid leadership at all costs?

When I look back, I can see that I was raised to be both a trusting follower of a few leaders ("don't ask questions, don't challenge, and don't doubt"), but also expected to be a leader in my family, my school, and my church. It's clear to me that I made some very serious decisions about leadership at an early age, and many of those decisions were the direct result of the messaging I received about it. With only two real options of leadership presented to me — selfish, deceitful, and power-hungry or selfless, honest, and sacrificial — I chose the latter and only followed those I believed embodied those qualities. However, there was just enough exposure to alternative leadership styles (ahem, rebels with an everyone-wins cause) in Robinhood, Ren (*Footloose*), and eventually Professor Keating (*Dead Poets Society*) that when

I was returned to the leadership path after many years of wandering, I wasn't about to just follow the trend and fit the formula.

When the inspiration for my message struck me like a lightning bolt, it came with a "vision of success," in which I was working side-by-side with successful thought leaders to change the world, had a book on the New York Times Bestseller list, and was making a ton of money and traveling the world with my family. It literally felt like I had met my Destiny. All of my experiences, expertise, natural talents, and even disappointments and failures suddenly alchemized into an opportunity to leave the world better than I found it. I was apparently born for this role of leadership. Primed to be a good student/follower, I dove headfirst into learning what it would take to be a messenger (yay!), a CEO (oh no, I have to look at spreadsheets!?!), and a leader (I definitely don't have my shit together enough for people to follow me!). Fortunately for me, Life was working on my behalf and surrounded me with leaders to help me along the way.

As I learned and mimicked successful messaging, business development, and leadership strategies, I discarded or adjusted approaches that didn't feel right to me. For the most part, I was successful and grew a business that was true to my intention. Unfortunately, right after I achieved one level of success, I faced two challenges that brought me to my knees and made me realize that I had more work to do before I could step into the next level.

Suddenly unable to access the Guidance that had helped me to that point, I sat on my meditation pillow for hours daily and begged for answers. It was during this time that

I stopped "using story to help Aaron learn and grow" and started to rely on it to give me the answers that seemed so hard to find. When he came home from school one day and said, "Mom, my friend is watching this show called *Merlin* and I wanna check it out," I began another type of schooling in leadership. The story of King Arthur and Merlin helped me to realize that my leadership was imbalanced, and that I needed to purge my "kingdom" of its previous paradigm of fear and manipulation. And then we found *Korra*, the cartoon sequel to *Avatar: The Last Airbender,* which literally gave me the pathway to healing my leadership wounds and stepping back into the role I believe I was made to fulfill. Even my old favorite, *Lord of The Rings*, served up a much-needed salve as I watched Theoden, King of Rohan, retreat from his duty because of his past failures and then, after a much-needed ass-kicking from another reluctant king, ride out to meet the enemy and truly protect his people.

I've been repeatedly inspired by Aang (*Avatar: The Last Airbender*) to do what must be done, but to find a way to accomplish it that doesn't compromise my moral code. I was reminded by Noah (*The Affair*) to keep a watchful eye on the parts of myself that have been wounded and starved for attention and acknowledgment, so that they don't inspire impulsive or compulsive behavior that destroys my life from the inside-out. Eugenia (*The Help*) reminded me that part of my leadership role on this planet is to expose the disgusting and disempowering ideas and systems that keep humanity (and particularly messengers and change-makers) from moving forward, and that it's a rather dangerous but necessary path. And Elsa (*Frozen 2*) made me smile when she tried to ignore the whisper on the wind that called her into the unknown, away from her home, and into the next level of her leadership. Of course I cried big alligator tears when I realized the message was to heal the generational traumas by exposing the truth of how they had unfolded. Most recently, Coach *Ted Lasso* provided a masterclass on the importance and power of seeing, centering, and trusting both the humanity and divinity in the people we lead, and never giving up on the internal work that true leadership always requires.

I'm so grateful for what Story has taught me about leadership, and I'm blessed to have walked this journey of reclaiming my leadership with my son in the front-row seat. Hopefully, he will learn not only from the mistakes of the heroes and villains on screen, but also mine, as he sets out to be the leader he was clearly destined to become.

I'll Do It My Way

I seriously didn't want to write this chapter. I spent a month procrastinating and wondering what was wrong with me until it finally came to me *why* I couldn't write it. It was right after the recording of an episode of our new podcast *Sips of Story 'n Sanity: The Stories Behind the Stories*.

Our guest that episode was Alyssa—my aunt, who's really actually more like an older sibling, if I'm honest. After we ended the recording, we chatted together for a few minutes. My mom mentioned the first part of the interview, during which she asked Alyssa what it's like to be only twenty-five years old and have all of these accomplishments in her bio. Alyssa's extremely honest response affirmed an idea my mom had been mulling over. She wanted to create a workshop where she would help people re/write their bio, and not just a good bio, but an honest one that is both relevant to their past and present accomplishments as well as near-future achievements that they haven't accepted or integrated quite yet. For example, someone who's about to publish a book for the first time will be able to call themselves an "author" in their bio and future marketing material, yet many people struggle with new titles like that—even when they've earned it.

After I heard my mom explain that people struggle to write their bios because, in doing so, they have to accept certain titles or identities, everything clicked.

The reason I didn't want to write this chapter is because in every other one, I tell a personal story of mine with real examples from my life related to the chapter's theme. And because this chapter is called leadership, well… I had to accept that *I was* and *am* a leader in some capacity. *Gulp.*

It was definitely a Merlin (*Merlin*) moment. Even when everyone knew he was destined to play a vital part in saving Camelot, he resisted stepping into that role until he had no other choice. The universe is funny that way.

I think that the word "leader" often comes across as an objective term used to describe a special ability to lead that is usually bestowed upon a single person. But what does it actually *mean* to be a "leader"? Who should get the title?

I personally see it as a malleable and subjective term that changes based on the beliefs and experiences of every individual, sort of like how people define "success." While there may be some commonality, many people have different definitions of what it means to be successful.

So what does it, or should it, mean to be a leader?

I actually believe leadership looks different than most might think. Stories have taught me that everyone has skills, talents, and experience to contribute to the "bigger picture." In other words, everyone can be a leader in their own way... if they choose to be.

In stories like *Harry Potter*, *Lord of the Rings*, and *Avatar: The Last Airbender*, comrades work together and use their unique skills to solve problems or save each other. Without Ron, Harry and Hermione (*Harry Potter and the Sorcerer's Stone*) would almost certainly have failed to win the game of Wizard's Chess and proceed to the next chamber. Without Toph or Zuko, Aang (*Avatar: The Last Airbender*) wouldn't have been able to learn the earth or fire bending he needed to defeat the Fire Lord. Without Merry and Pippin (*Lord of the Rings*) convincing Treebeard and the other Ents to protect their forest from Saruman, Isengard wouldn't have been destroyed, which would have given the upper hand to Sauron and the orcs.

Even though these stories may have a central "hero" or leader, *everybody* had the opportunity to lead and contribute to the goal at hand. Everyone had a purpose and a skillset vital to, well... saving the world.

And even though our quests may not be as grand, we must also accept who we are and be a leader when we are called to be. I know that's a strange sentiment, but it's become a truth in my life.

I never really saw myself as a leader until now, even though my mom has always told me she sees leadership qualities in me. It took me laying out and reviewing all of the things I have done recently and am currently doing to admit it. It's true. I've been a leader in a lot of ways. And what I know now is that when we are called to contribute who we are to a greater cause, we are leading. We may not be *THE* leader, but rather *A* leader.

So, why was the title of "leader" so unreasonably "sticky" to me? Well, I think the most obvious reason is that the title comes with a lot of weight and responsibility, depending on the capacity in which we're being a leader, which varies by situation. But that's not the biggest reason—for me, anyway. The prospect of greater responsibilities never really irks me. Do you know how many people have jokingly asked me to run for president one day? That's probably part-in-parcel of having been given so much responsibility while young. Seriously, Mom made me solely responsible for a puppy at age six and showed me how to make my school lunches in third grade. So, no, it's not responsibility that's at issue.

However, thinking back on how I've been jokingly asked to run for president got me thinking; and I realized that at about the same time I was stepping into what most would call "leadership roles," I started paying attention to politics.

In other words, that's when I began to notice how our nation's *leaders* straight-out lie, defame their opponents, and act like hypocrites at every corner. I think we can all agree that many of the leaders that are talked about in the news and are frequently at the forefront of our minds do some crappy things. Why would I want to be a leader if they look, sound, and act like that? And that's not the only place I had seen terrible leaders and the impact they have on those they are supposed to be serving.

King Runeard (*Frozen 2*), Elsa and Anna's grandfather, was always viewed as a great leader to the people of Arendelle. As we later learn, however, he was really a tyrant in disguise. He lied to and tricked the Northuldra into accepting a dam intended to harm their land and launching a surprise-attack during a diplomatic gathering. Cersei (*Game of Thrones*), on the other hand, did not pretend to be anything other than the power-hungry control-freak that she was.

Then I began to notice that even leaders who are trying their best to do the right thing fall into an old pattern of destruction. Kaleesi (*Game of Thrones*) had great intentions, but ended up destroying the kingdom she claimed to be the rightful heir to and had an interest in protecting. After all the good she did, she just lost her damn mind and destroyed everything she had been working for.

Ahhh… that's why it's sticky. The leaders that I pay attention to are terrible examples.

Now I see my error in focusing so much of my attention and energy on the not-so-ideal leaders and less on the ones in my life that I get to witness be incredible leaders in their own right on a daily basis.

Every day, so many people are doing their best to be good people and use their innate gifts and talents to lead the world in a better direction. *That's* leadership, and that's who I *want* to be and what I *want* to do.

And I think that's what I've been working toward in one way or another over the last few years.

I started by claiming the reins of my educational journey, which led to the honing of several leadership skills, beginning with an ethics debate class where I learned speaking and persuasion skills (not to mention how to even begin to look at and think through tough ethical decisions). Then, of course, I joined Mock Trial where I learned a whole lot about our judicial system and how to perform under a lot of pressure. A year later, I became a co-editor for my school's paper and oversaw record publishing in both article and issue count. Outside of my education, I jumped at the chance to help a family friend with the techy side of her online events; and while I was there, I witnessed her teach educators and school district staff how to self-regulate and take care of themselves so they could lead at full capacity. Suddenly, I had tools to manage my energy, cultivate the best qualities in others, and create spaces where everyone feels safe. (I'm sure this was just a coincidence!)

Around the same time, I helped to establish a youth advisory council for a network aimed at providing young people with mentors and opportunities to aid in unfolding their potential; and today, in cooperation with that same network, I'm working with other leaders to deliver an online learning community platform for students and their families in New Mexico.

So yeah, I'm leading stuff with other incredible leaders, and recent years have no doubt prepared me for the position I'm in today and the possibilities of the near-future. And honestly, it's not as scary as I thought it'd be. In fact, it's really exciting, even when it's not for others. My mom's gonna have a little panic attack with me writing this here, but I think it's my duty to do my part in manifesting it into existence… or something like that. Publishing house, anyone? As my mom has repeatedly said every time the prospect of creating a publishing house is mentioned, "Eeek!"

I think the part of my situation that I overlook the most is simultaneously the biggest blessing, and it's that I get to lead *my* way. I'm not trying to fit anyone's mold for being a leader, nor do I want to. I've witnessed too many people in my life try to copy "the formulas," and I've watched enough movies and TV to know where that road leads.

President Coin (*The Hunger Games*) claimed to be a new kind of leader that would leave the Capitol's sins in the past; but as soon as she claimed power, she tried to restart the Hunger Games, using the children of Capitol as reparations—following the formula and pattern of fear to shame and control the old rulers. Good thing Katniss saw straight through that mess and ended that horrible story loop.

I think Aang (*Avatar: The Last Airbender*) got it right when he was trying to figure out how to defeat the Fire Lord. He didn't want to kill him because doing so was against his airbender philosophy. Exploring his options, Aang called the spirits of previous Avatars to lend him insight and advice as to how to solve the problem, and most of them told him he would have to kill his enemy. Thankfully, he was determined and found his own way to defeat the Fire Lord without compromising his values—he took his bending away.

What if it were that easy? I mean, of course it's not easy to be a leader; but what if it were easier? And what if what made it easier was taking the time to sort through what we have learned about leadership, to decide which models to follow and which ones to avoid, and to commit to leading our own life *our* way.

It's just me and my Co-Author—as my mom calls It—at the wheel, taking me down a path ain't nobody's ever seen.

This son of mine. Of course he tossed in that short but provocative sentence about a publishing company.

You see, there is one small part of this young man's leadership journey that he left out completely. Since he could talk, he has been thinking way ahead of me, calling forth more of my potential, and holding me accountable to it all. A leader indeed.

A born entrepreneur, he's been curious about my business since pre-school; and I've been very candid about it all—the ups, the downs, the uglies... the failures and the successes. At some point, I paid him to do little jobs for me—filing papers, inputting contacts into my CRM, etc. As he got older and developed mad technical skills, he became my go-to for all computer glitches. But in between all of those tasks, his intuitive and poignant questions were inspiring bigger dreams, offerings, and impact.

So, when he told me he wanted to try the path of internships instead of go to college, I wasn't surprised at all. I proposed that he start working with one of my clients who needed a virtual assistant while he figured out his next steps. Of course, he got into her business and did what he'd been doing with mine for years: "Mom, you know, if we used this software, it would help us…" and "Why is she using this? This over here is a less expensive option and performs better…" Eventually, she asked him to build an online community; and when I looked at what he had built, I was reminded of a dream I had nine years ago — an online community that would be a place for healing and integration. A few weeks later, he had set up CocoonU and organized my work into one place where people could access it easily.

Realizing this was something he enjoyed, he started a business called Caterbuilder — clearly his destiny! — and I began to bring him in on more contracts, which allowed me to expand my services to help clients with stuff I never would have tackled on my own.

But something funny was happening for me behind the scenes as well. At almost the exact same time he was building Caterbuilder, I was receiving the same message from multiple sources. One week, the astrologist said, "Your dharma is collaborative leadership, Amanda. That's what you are made for — not to work alone." A few days later, a coach I talk to once a year was telling me, "Amanda, it's time to stop doing this on your own. And from what you said about Aaron and Alyssa, you already have a team."

Wut? I already had a team? I was already leading? Yep, that's right. He came by all that honestly.

So, I decided to do it consciously. Suddenly, we were having weekly team meetings with two clients-turned-friends who wanted to be part of the expansion. And then almost immediately, we were working on multiple new projects and launching a podcast and a collaborative book together. And now, yes, we are looking at creating a publishing company because well... all signs are pointing in that direction.

It's been a magical but rather messy year. Not only am I trying to figure out how to delegate and hold people accountable, I'm doing all of this uncomfortable new stuff with family members and friends. In one way, there's more grace; in another, the stakes are much higher.

We are operating in The Unknown and navigating Uncertainty and all that it brings up for us... together. We are deepening our Self-Knowledge of our superpowers and kryptonite... together. We are Training and being mentored by each other and by others who want to help... together. We are Comrades, deciding how best to leverage all of our superpowers for the good of the vision and figuring out how to keep our kryptonite from taking down the whole team and culture... together. We are actively working to hold the space for Redemption of all of our parts, and those of our clients... together. We are following the breadcrumbs of Destiny and taking big chances... together. And, we are clearly all stepping into truer Leadership of our own lives and the arenas in which we are asked to serve... together.

Story has given me some very clear guidance and warnings around Leadership; and on the days when I feel overwhelmed by the weight of responsibility every leader carries, two powerful scenes from *Merlin* remind me of what is really important: being the type of leader who inspires simply through how I move through the world, staying true to the vision they have experienced and want to help me expand, and making certain that I continue looking them in the eyes and honoring the magic that they bring.

The young King Arthur invited his knights to a round table, actively demonstrating his belief in their character and their capacity to lead with him collaboratively. "Are there any around this table that would join me?" In response to his question, the knights stand one by one and not only declare their devotion but the reason for it. He had taught them through his model what it meant to be a good leader. He had been willing to sacrifice his own life for them several times. He had treated them like *people* more than subjects or employees. Their unanimous answer was summed up in the promise of one: "I believe in the world you will build."

But Arthur wasn't perfect. Despite all his progressive thinking and integrity-driven action, he was blind to the fact that the young servant boy who attended to his menial daily tasks, who he regularly teased and taunted, was actually a young magician who was regularly saving his ass. For five seasons, viewers like me wondered how long it would take for this leader to see that he could not be who he was meant to be without this person. When we got our answer, I was a blubbering mess. (Spoiler alert!) Arthur is mortally wounded and Merlin is trying to save his life. After several years of hiding his true identity (because magick was against the law) and suffering the young king's arrogance and ignorance, the young magician had to expose his superpowers to Arthur in order to help him save the kingdom. In their final

interactions, the wound in Arthur's physical body seems
much less painful than the awakening of who this young man
really is and all that he has done despite how poorly he was
treated. "That was you who...? Wait, were you also the one
who...? But I..." Dumbfounded, the young king resigns to the
truth as his body resigns to the wound, and his last words
are those of a true leader: "Everything you've done, I know
now. For me. For Camelot. For the kingdom you helped me
build... I want to say something I've never said to you before:
Thank you."

Thanks to Story and every amazing leader I've ever
met, I know that true leadership is not only seeing and
communicating a powerful vision, but calling forth the
magic and potential in others to make it so *and* making sure
they know that *you know* the kingdom would never be built
without their contribution and you wouldn't want it to be.

Diving Deeper into Leadership
with Your Kids and Their Stories

I'm a Leader, Too

When you think of leaders in the world, who are the people that immediately enter your mind? Maybe they're a pop culture icon. Maybe they're your boss. Maybe they're a politician, a religious leader, or a famous scholar.

But how do you define a leader? Better yet, how do you define a *good* leader?

Answers to these questions vary and tend to cater to the respondent's outlook upon the world. Some people think a good leader is someone that inspires action. Others believe good leaders are brave and commanding forces that get things done. Visionary, honest, focused, compassionate, communicative; all words we've heard that are used to describe a great leader.

But what if there's more? What if the most unsuspecting, inexperienced, naïve, shy, and scarred individuals were to discover who they were and learn how to harness their unique superpowers to save the world? Could they be leaders, too?

Aang (*Avatar: The Last Airbender*) and his friends were mostly normal teenagers with burdensome and complicated histories. Throughout the series, we get to see them reconcile with the past and heal old wounds while they train to become masters of the elements and leaders of a plan to save the world. Each member of Team Avatar used their unique strengths and abilities to defeat foes, save each other from treacherous situations, and clear the obstacles standing between them and their destinations.

P.T. Barnum (*The Greatest Showman*) brought together a group of misfits to contribute their talent toward the greater goals of putting on a show and making people smile. Although society didn't see them as desirable or capable of greatness, their individual strengths were brought together for a collective goal that required bravery, vision, and trust.

Two content hobbits (*The Lord of the Rings*) were roped into the journey of a lifetime; and through their perseverance, sacrifice, and commitment to the possibility of a brighter future, they became the greatest unsuspecting heroes and leaders of their time. In the end, after their treacherous task was complete, the new king honored their leadership and selfless actions with the words: "You bow to no one."

Regardless of circumstance or belief, it is possible for every one of us to become leaders. Sure, most of us probably won't become politicians or religious leaders — but that's not what being a leader is about. Fostering and contributing our natural talents and unique skills toward common goals is how we can become the leaders of our own lives and create positive change, even if that change is a small change in our family or our small community.

Which stories can open conversations around leadership? Think beyond the Disney Kings and Queen and territories and subject; explore how characters first become the leaders of their lives (or fail to).

Merlin was our gateway into the leadership conversation, and while it was extremely powerful to see such intensely different leadership styles (collaborative Arthur and his tyrannical father), there was very little wrestling with the challenges and subtleties of leadership. So, we took the plunge and started *Game of Thrones* with Aaron in his mid-teens. Whew! That was a whole lot of violence and skin in that first season — a great way to hook viewers to deliver what we believe is a really important message. As it has already been said, Circe was like the devil incarnate, but we had high hopes for Kahleesi — that she would be able to avoid her father's fate. Contrasted with the arc of John Snow's story of humble beginnings and aspirations, there was a lot of good opportunity for discussing what compels and sustains true and empowering leaders. But this was about leadership of a kingdom, and we wanted something that would address self-leadership so we could discuss why and how leaders crumble under pressures and temptations. *The Greatest Showman* provided a smaller scope on the same conversation, but after we realized the wound of "not enough," we decided we should explore this on a more mundane level. So, we did a crazy thing and turned on *The Affair*. A man in his fifties, with just about everything he wants externally, gets a little too excited by a young waitress at the small-town diner during his family vacation. The viewer gets the opportunity to watch the self-deception that has to take place in order for him to follow through on his desire, and then witness the impact of a moment of lost self-leadership turn into utter destruction in his marriage, his family, and his career. As we traveled the road of destruction and then redemption with him, we began to understand that it was an unmet need for significance that caused him to sacrifice everything for a fleeting glimpse of it.

Obviously, content like this is not for the young children, but we share it with you here to give you a very clear example of a leadership conversation that we believe our culture must have *and* the discomfort it may require for us to have it. Our children will likely never be crowned king/queen, and some of them will never experience building and leading a vision and team; but all of them need to realize that they are leaders *of their own lives* and that their choices as leaders of their own lives impact their loved ones, friends, communities, etc.

I Have to Do It My Way

The way in which a leader came to power and why they chose to be a leader is paramount to understanding the type of change they created, whether it be intentionally or unintentionally.

Throughout history and within many stories lies what we believe to be an extremely important truth, and that is this: The best leaders are the ones that don't want power and/or have nothing to gain from it.

When Jon Snow (*Game of Thrones*) found out that he was the rightful king of Westeros, he didn't want to accept that responsibility. In contrast, Khaleesi claimed that *she* was the rightful heir to the Iron Throne and actively wanted to become the queen.

The tale of Jon Snow is parodied by the story of George Washington's election as the first President of the United States. The adulation and expectations of the American people, Washington feared, were too great for him to live up to. Instead, he desired a quiet life away from celebrity.[1] Yet, he bore the burden of fostering the infant nation for eight years, and while an imperfect man, he laid the groundwork for future generations to improve and further embody the Founding Fathers' initial convictions of freedom and equality for all.

Another truth that we believe to be archetypally relevant and universal throughout both history and stories is the idea that those who fight out of hate, spite, and revenge are doomed to fail when contending with those who fight out of love, hope, and a righteous vision for the future.

Khaleesi (*Game of Thrones*) began fighting for the Iron Throne because she loved her people and wanted to set them free; but over time, her goal became one of vengeance and retribution rather than love and justice. Merlin (*Merlin*) trained and strived to protect Arthur and the ideals that

---

[1]   https://www.smithsonianmag.com/history/george-washington-the-reluc-
       tant-president-49492/

he stood for, while their enemies were driven by their hatred for Camelot and a lust for revenge on Arthur and the Pendragon family. Korra (*The Legend of Korra*) followed through on her duty as the Avatar to maintain balance and protect all people, including the benders of Republic City, whereas Aman hated all benders and sought to destroy or disempower them.

And throughout history, as depicted in the French, American, and Russian (February Revolution) revolutions, people who fought against their governments weren't just fighting against tyranny. They were fighting *for* a better future by demanding freedom and more democratic institutions.

The heroes of these stories had a goal, an idea, or a people — a northern star, if you will — that they aimed to embody or protect. On the other hand, while the villains may have also had a "northern star," the difference between them was this: The heroes fought *for* something while the villains fought *against* something.

As you watch leaders in your favorite stories AND in real life — teachers, pastors, businessmen, politicians, etc. — wonder out loud with your child about what might drive that person.

What are the clues that this person is really operating for The Good of those they serve, or the signs that maybe they have fallen prey to a lust for power, position, money, etc.?

No, this isn't about teaching children to make snap judgments about people and leadership. It's about developing their attention to details, clues, and themes and patterns associated with empowering leadership and those associated with disempowering leadership. Remember, if we can help them to separate the worth of the person from their behavior and character, then all we are doing is teaching them how to be more discerning and wise leaders and community members.

Choosing My Own Path

Part of being a leader is making tough and consequential decisions; and through those decisions, they carve their own path by answering this question (or a similar one): Are we going to do the old thing or the new thing?

Choosing between the ways of the past and the possibility of creating a new paradigm is no easy feat, especially when that decision could affect countless people for generations to come. A burden such as this is not for the faint of heart, and requires self-reflection and a commitment to do what's in the world's best interest as well as yours.

So what should you choose? We can't give you the answer, but we know some stories that might help.

On a fast-track journey to achievement, P.T. Barnum (*The Greatest Showman*) lost his way and abandoned his allies. He fell into a cycle of believing his popularity and wealth was "never enough;" and instead of listening to and honoring his friends that got him to such a place of fame and success, he became "blinded by the lights" and turned his back on them. Luckily, he eventually realized that everything he ever wanted or needed was his all along, and that this camaraderie was more valuable to him than fame and what society had deemed as "success." He chose loyalty and love over the patterns of greed and despair in which he almost lost himself. He chose the new way over the old way.

In Neo's (*The Matrix*) case, he consciously chose the new way even when the consequences of his decision weren't exactly clear to him. He chose the red pill (the new way: waking up) over the blue pill (the old way: life as usual).

Hours before Avatar Aang (*Avatar: The Last Airbender*) was destined to face Fire Lord Ozai, he realized that in order to defeat the Fire Lord, he was expected to take his life. As an Air Nomad, this conflicted with Aang's deeply held beliefs that every life is sacred; and even though Lord Ozai was by no means what many might call a "good man," Aang simply could not accept that he would have to kill him, even though the spirits of his previous Avatars insisted that he would have to set aside his beliefs for the good of the world. Determined to find another way, he acquired the help of an ancient Lion Turtle who eventually bestowed Aang with a special power that he used to take Ozai's fire bending powers away without killing him, rendering him completely powerless instead. In the end, Aang forged a new way that was both right for him and the world.

But not everyone chooses the new way in the end.

In the final weeks of the war, Khaleesi (*Game of Thrones*) slowly distanced herself from the new way that she promised to bring about after multiple tragedies befell her. Eventually, intentionally or not, she chose the old way by burning King's Landing to the ground and terrorizing the people she originally wanted to protect.

Even though she so badly wanted the new way, she wasn't strong enough to stay the course.

Which stories will you use to spark conversations about old and new ways of creating change in the world?

What are some of the ways people have gone about leadership and change before that simply do not feel good to your child?

What characters will allow you to explore the "why" and "how" of leadership — to discuss the age-old "means versus ends" dilemma? Is it okay or even effective to go against your principles for the greater good?

These are some of the most challenging conversations we've had, largely because the explorations have exposed some old wounds and anger toward leaders who hurt us or led us astray; but all of these conversations have put Leadership in the larger context of the hero's journey. When we see each other struggling, we wonder about the Uncertainty that's got the other all bunched up. When we hear anger about disempowering leaders and paradigms, we revisit the themes of Redemption. As you discuss Leadership with your children, wonder out loud about the connections with the other themes and then listen and be amazed.

Accountability
Sometimes leaders get off-track and lose sight of their original goals or promises. In a world full of uncertainties and suffering, it can be hard to stay true to who we are as a leader. Loyal friends and allies are required to remind leaders of their commitments and to hold them accountable.

Part of getting off-track can mean that we abandon the people who helped us get to where we are. In an extreme case, Jaime Lannister (*Game of Thrones*) begged his sister, Cersei Lannister, to send their army to the Wall and defend Westeros from the White Walkers. This would have required their army to fight alongside their own enemies against the looming and catastrophic invasion of the White Walkers. She refused, and in doing so, abandoned her relationship with Jaime. Even though Jaime would have done almost anything for her — even murder — she nearly had Jaime killed for treason, but couldn't bring herself to give the order. She turned her back on her one true love, her most loyal servant, and her own kingdom. And like we mentioned before, P.T. Barnum (*The Greatest Showman*) became "blinded by the lights" of fame and left his friends (who helped him become famous) behind in their time of need. Later, he realized that his relationships were more important to him than any amount of fame, wealth, or power. After this realization, he fought as hard as he could to win back the people he loved.

Sometimes, the abandonment isn't selfish, but rather selfless, in an attempt to protect the people they care about. In *Avatar: The Last Airbender* and *Harry Potter*, both Aang and Harry tried saving the world by themselves so as to not put their friends in danger — but their friends loved them too much to let that happen. They stuck together and got each other "back on the right track" when someone got lost in the uncertainty and almost fell to temptation.

There are also a lot of instances where there is an unseen, invisible person who's making it possible for a leader to do what they're meant to do... without getting killed. Part of that person's job often includes keeping the leader accountable and on the "right track," too. Arthur (*Merlin*) was one such leader who was being aided and guided by Merlin, who went largely unrecognized for what he did to help Arthur become who he was meant to be. Merlin so deeply believed in Arthur's vision for Camelot and his compassion for his people that he was willing to be unseen and unappreciated. The same principle is true in *Star Trek: The Next Generation* with First Officer William Riker. While he wasn't nearly as "unseen" or "invisible" as Merlin was, his role as second-in-command to Captain Picard was vital to the survival of the ship and others that the crew were tasked to protect.

Loyal, competent, and strong "second-in-commands" are crucial for any "first-in-command." Not only do they fiercely protect their leader, but they also hold them accountable and ensure that their intentions are reflected in the work they do and not corrupted by nefarious actors or trauma.

Quests can't be completed, goals can't be reached, and change can't manifest if leaders don't have a support structure. Great leaders always surround themselves with people that protect and advise them, but they must also be open to being called out and held accountable whenever they stray from the "right track."

For those of us leaders who are not easily "blinded by the lights," we may find ourselves blinded by old wounds, especially when they collide with similar wounds in others. In *Ted Lasso,* we see a true leader who is more concerned about the humans he is leading than the outcomes they achieve together; and in the middle of season two (spoiler alert!), we discover that it is a childhood wound that has made him great at making people feel seen. Regardless of whether they write his check every month or wash the dirty towels, Coach Ted makes the people around him feel known and cared for until his childhood pain is triggered and sets off a series of panic attacks. While he sets about to address his problems rather heroically, he still manages to do his job so well that even the audience doesn't realize until it's too late that he has left someone on his team (with a similar father wound) feeling abandoned and unloved to the point of betrayal. Even the best leaders are imperfect humans who will make mistakes; but they are also the ones who will be brave enough to confront "painful pasts," take responsibility, make amends, and continuously strive to become better versions of themselves. They inspire those they lead to trust themselves and their own leadership capacity: "Don't listen to me... You just listen to your gut, okay? And on your way down to your gut, check in with your heart. Between those two things, they'll let you know what's what. They make good harmony..."

Finally, and maybe most importantly, we can learn from Coach Ted's best efforts that it is not enough to make people feel seen; we have to also remind them that we are humans full of blind spots and invite them to take responsibility and be accountable for their well-being too, and join us at a round table to address their concerns and grievances before they become darkened by resentment. This is the only way we can be the leaders in the world that we are meant to be — leaders who cultivate other leaders.

Which examples of healthy, loving accountability can you point to in your children's stories?

Explore the "why" and "how" of accountability with your child. What are the most (and least) effective strategies for holding leaders accountable? Why do they work (or not work)?

Did anyone ever teach you that loving accountability was a thing, let alone how to do it? Most of us didn't get that memo, and this is an absolute life-changing concept to give a child early in life. We do have to warn you though. When you help your children learn how to do this, be ready for them to try it with you. Oh yeah. Get ready for it. Take those deep breaths, thank them for their feedback and make whatever amends are necessary, and then help them refine their approach for next time.

This Is Fine

Spoiler: it's actually not fine. And that's okay.
What we are about to reveal to you is a secret as old as humankind. It's been kept so secret and sacred among the highest ranks of leaders that there are very few who are privy to its truth and profound wisdom. And that secret is this: Most leaders don't have their shit together, so get used to it.

Right, maybe that's not very secret. But the value of its wisdom is still profound.

We don't know a single leader in the world that has it "all together," even though many may pretend or appear to "have it together." Some people are just really good at hiding their baggage, and some are not.

Hours before the invasion of the Fire Nation, Aang (*Avatar: The Last Airbender*) was... well, he was freaking out. He was about to storm the capital of the Fire Nation with an army at his command in the hopes of defeating the Fire Lord. With the stress of anticipation infecting his mind, he had frequent nightmares and couldn't sleep. He started spending his days and nights training, strategizing, and losing his mind to sleep deprivation. Of course, he told everyone that he was fine, but it was quite obvious that he was not.

He even started having hallucinations about how his lemur and flying bison were fighting each other like samurais as the country-side sheep observed and started dancing in circles. That's pretty bad.

And in the Netflix show *Good Girls*, three moms always pretend to have it together, but really never do (What mom does? Sorry, Mom...). They get caught up in several crime syndicates throughout the series and end up stuck in a never-ending cycle of moral dilemmas they must conquer for the sake of their safety and their families' safety.

But what makes great leaders so incredible and vital to the world is that, even when things get tough and they don't "have it together," they willingly choose to confront the unknown in the face of infinite uncertainty.

Elsa's journey in *Frozen 2* is a great example of this confrontation. Even though she had her kingdom in order, a voice called her out into the unknown. Obedient to the call to leadership, she uncovered old wounds that her ancestors inflicted on neighboring peoples and found a way to unify them, all while saving her kingdom from a flood.

In contrast, leaders who are afraid of making mistakes and confronting the uncertain future will inevitably lead their followers into despair. After being released from his curse, King Théoden of Rohan (*The Lord of the Rings*) chose to bring his people into Helm's Deep rather than confront the approaching enemy. He felt as though his people had suffered enough due to him being unwittingly controlled by the enemy. Ultimately, he allowed regret and fear to guide his decision. He ignored his advisors who told him that their best chance was to confront the enemy head-on as opposed to hiding, and he simply couldn't believe that neighboring kingdoms would be willing to aid them in their time of need.

Leaders and heroes aren't just heralded for making the right decisions. Rather, they are celebrated for their ability to make tough decisions (both right and wrong) and not let fear and uncertainty cloud their judgment.

What stories will provide opportunities to discuss the challenging realities of leadership, and what to do when they emerge?

Which leader characters will help you to cultivate respect and sympathy for imperfect leaders, and let your children know that it's more than okay to be transparent, human, imperfect leaders?

Maybe you can even find a character that will show them that imperfect leaders who take responsibility are even more powerful than others?

The truth is, you are raising a leader. You wouldn't have picked up this book if you were not a born leader yourself, and born leaders raise powerful leaders. Our hope is that this book will help you enjoy a more fun and powerful way to cultivate the character of your little leader and empower them with the wisdom to preserve their freedom and that of those they love and serve.

Sam: "It's like in the great stories, Mr. Frodo. The ones that really mattered. Full of darkness and danger they were. And sometimes you didn't want to know the end... because how could the end be happy? How could the world go back to the way it was when so much bad had happened? But in the end, it's only a passing thing... this shadow. Even darkness must pass."

Frodo: "What are we holding on to, Sam?"

Sam: "That there's some good in this world, Mr. Frodo. And it's worth fighting for."

~ J.R.R. Tolkien, The Two Towers ~

Conclusion

Raised By Story

My phone buzzed and lit up while I sat at my desk—I definitely needed a break from the trivial tasks I was working on. I picked up my phone and viewed the screen to find a lone news notification: "Sky News: Black Lives Matter: Federal agents confront protesters in Portland." It was July of 2020, and the unrest over the death of George Floyd was at its peak. I could feel the stress creep into my body, so I let out a heavy sigh to relieve the pressure, opened the notification, and watched the video that began to play.

"Federal agents sent to restore order in Portland have poured petrol on disorder. What was a largely peaceful protest has escalated into violence. The main battle line is here: outside the federal courthouse."

The news outlet played a clip of protestors rattling the fence that surrounded the once-recognizable Hatfield Federal Courthouse—the same one I had set foot in not too long before this time for the 2020 Oregon State Mock Trial Competition.

"Protestors unable to pull down the new fence throw fireworks over." A loud explosion of white and red fireworks filled the entrance lined with grand and heavily-graffitied columns.

"Teargas is fired back. Many here are prepared for this, but as federal agents emerge in their dozens, those in gas masks run, too. Rubber bullets fired into the darkness." More booms and screams echoed from down a downtown street. "It's quite frightening."

Surrounded by masked protestors and thick clouds of teargas, the reporter who had been narrating over the hectic clips appeared on screen. You could see the courthouse in the background across the street. The light of emergency vehicles flashed behind her, alarms blaring, cars struggling to move at the nearby stoplight. The reporter was sporting a backpack, a black helmet, and her own gas mask that muffled her voice as she spoke into the microphone.

"This isn't the first time teargas has been fired at protesters tonight, but it's the first time we've seen federal agents outside of the federal courthouse; and it's the first time it's driven crowds away. But it doesn't look like they've gone—" a deafening boom silenced her last word. Her eyes flinched, and without so much as a pause, she picked up again. "Certainly, it doesn't seem like either side is going to give up any time soon."

As I digested what I had just watched, all I could think was, *When will our country—and our world—be able to catch its breath? Will we ever be able to work this out? Is it possible to take a freaking break from all of the chaos and the uncertainty that has ravaged our nation, not just since COVID began, but the four years preceding? Is healing possible? Has the world gone mad?!*

My mom would often come home from her part-time job working the register at Whole Foods and tell stories of toilet paper shortages, arguments over masks, old and particularly at-risk people being terrified for their health, and military folks being unfettered in their discourse about how much they worried about our freedom. No wonder we were experiencing upset and upheaval beyond our private lives. The collective had just been thrown into the deep end of uncertainty and was drowning in a perpetual state of fear, preserved by never-ending tragedy beyond what many people had ever experienced in their lives.

I was one of those many people. My learning community, of course, shut down. I was disconnected again like I had been three years earlier, triggering all of my inflexibility instincts that I had to wrestle once again. Our family and friends had been affected worse than us financially and health-wise. We were incredibly blessed, but I was rattled.

Why were so many awful things happening? How could I stay happy and stable in the midst of all this?

Once the reality hit that this whole COVID situation was going to be an issue for the foreseeable future, I decided it was time to structure and sort out my life the best I could by using my superpowers. I made routine a necessity and planned my time better, I exercised more, and I found ways to continually stay curious in the online and technology space without disappearing from reality. Not only that, but I started *paying attention* to the world outside my own. I researched and explored, questioned and debated. I found ways to integrate what I had learned about bias, journalism, and of course, story, to come to my own conclusions through measured analysis and scrutiny.

I listened closely to a few people (distant mentors) for their courage and thoughtfulness, and listened to others from afar—not because I disagreed with their politics, but because of their closed-mindedness or style of analysis. I listened to people who I thought had strong foundational principles that undergirded their beliefs after scrutinizing for hypocrisy. It was more important to me that they were consistent in their messages and beliefs than whether or not I actually agreed with them. I can dismantle and evaluate others' messages and beliefs for myself, but I struggle to listen when I detect incongruity or dishonesty.

Soon enough, a Zoom group of Allies—close friends and family—banded together on a weekly basis to share information and support each other through the difficult time. I found my role as a heavy researcher and "memory bank" of news, openly questioning (and cringing at) narratives I thought to be false.

Like so many, the group explored thoughts and feelings around who the villains were through this. Who's responsible? Is it Trump? Is it China? Or is it nobody's fault? Is it Derek Chauvin, the officer who knelt on George Floyd's neck and back? Or the protestors who battered courthouses and burnt down police precincts? How could we not look for something or someone to blame for COVID, for injustice, for the deep divisions in our country? How could this happen to the world? To *us*?

Tough questions became tough conversations, and tough conversations became a more complete picture of what "the truth" is. And with a whole lot of pain and truth comes awakening. All that I knew and witnessed catalyzed new parts of me that I hadn't known before. The ignorant bystander became the citizen who couldn't wait to vote. The quiet pacifier became the hearty orator who says what he thinks. The simple-living follower became the self-assured driver who is more willing to lead.

Just two years ago, I had little desire to be in politics; and I still strongly dislike most politicians. But if things continue going to hell in a handbasket and I end up feeling called to serve in any capacity, I'm ready to stand up.

My mind has never been more primed to get involved and problem-solve whenever there is a need. It's no longer a solo mission, either—stepping in to lead individuals and teams with my superpowers gets easier by the day. No more worries, no more imposter syndrome, and no more taking a backseat... even for the small things.

Uncertainty, self-knowledge, training, camaraderie, redemption, destiny, and leadership: all themes and experiences that are embedded in my life story, and yours as well. Different periods of time bring forth or call for varying amounts of each, and these last couple years have brought forth so much uncertainty that needed to be balanced out by the others. Because of my story perspective, I wasn't destroyed by fear, anxiety, depression, or just outright hard choices; instead, I was compelled by curiosity, concern, compassion, and purpose. I jumped in to create a better situation as best I could, even when times were darkest. In fact, I became a better version of myself.

In a way, all that's transpired has happened *for* me, not *to* me. I refused to submit to victimhood and blame, and instead, forged a path with what I had. Turns out, it's exactly what I needed.

Is this what's happening on a grand scale, too? Is this happening for us? And if so, how can this story-based perspective help us get unstuck and keep moving forward? What if we could get our narratives right, know our villains from heroes, collect the right allies, use our superpowers in the highest and best way, choose leadership roles that light us up, and for goodness sake, stay the hell away from our kryptonite?

It was April 2020 (during the lockdown) when we were finishing one of the last episodes of *God Friended Me*, a show about a young atheist in New York who starts receiving hints from "God" via social media, and I looked over at my mom. "You know why this show—even though it is so cheesy sometimes—is the best show on tv?" She smiled back at me and waited for my answer. "Because it's one of the only shows that assumes that Life is happening *for* us, not *to* us."

I could see her heart getting caught in her throat as she nodded at me.

"It's just such a better perspective on life. What if we all just expected that the good stuff and the hard stuff was all happening to help us get to some sort of happy ending?"

"Life is happening *for* us, not *to* us" has become the lens through which I strive to view and live my life. Over the last five years (at least!), this concept has been one of the primary ideas with which I've wrestled. It's a hard one to swallow for many, including me just five odd years ago at a time when my life had been uprooted and my future felt more than uncertain.

Ironically, I was pretty freakin' fed up with the cliche, "everything happens for a reason," even though I heard my mom tell stories of clients' journeys being supported in inexplicably magical ways. What was happening for my mom's clients was undeniably divine, but I just couldn't understand why what I felt was happening *to* me was so much crappier than what was happening *for* everyone else.

Why isn't this happening for me, too? Why is everyone else happier than me? How do they know what they want to do? I want to be excited about life again.

What I believe truly killed my motivation to step up and change my life was the fact that I had become so utterly disconnected from who I was that I had completely lost sight of who I could be. I didn't know who I was anymore in Oregon. My identity felt stripped and left to dry, and then thrown in a volcano... kinda like Smeagol (*The Lord of the Rings*). The only way back to *me* was to discover myself again. To fight for myself again. To completely rewrite myself and my story.

Thank goodness my mom and I had watched countless heroes do this!

My mom no doubt saw my burnt-out spirit crawling its way through online public school, and how inflamed and unhealthy my body was. I felt crushed under the weight of nothingness and my lack of aspirations to be or do something…anything, really. But most of all, I think—no, I know—that my mom saw all of the good and powerful that I had forgotten and the future that I could create. She always has.

Over the next few months, I noticed her attempts to uncover what it was that I needed to thrive, whether I knew what "that" was or not. She tried to find out more about what I wanted to do and didn't, what lit me up and tore me down, and what or who I looked up to. Most important of all, she asked questions. *Lots* of questions. But once she knew what it was that my body and spirit needed, she set the intentions with me.

"We'll figure out why you're/I'm so inflamed."

"Let's find a better school with incredible mentors."

"I know there's a community out there where you'll feel that you belong."

And with the help of my family and my Co-Author, otherwise known as "The Head Honcho Upstairs" (or God, or The Universe, or Source, if you prefer), I was able to start what felt like not just a new chapter, but a completely new book in the story of my life.

Those intentions became reality in a matter of months. I started a diet that revealed to me that a minor allergic reaction to gluten and dairy was keeping me inflamed even though I didn't eat too much (not more than the average teenage boy, certainly). And as you've seen throughout this book, I found a homeschooling community that cultivated my deepest passions and pushed me to become open, flexible, and unapologetically happy. I found purpose in the community that this school provided me, and another community that fostered what had flourished at school by helping me articulate my core values, my strengths, and what I wanted to do in the world that is aligned with who I am. Every step of the way, I have been presented with more and more opportunities to carve my own path and follow my heart. Although, sometimes I find that I have to suspend my desires and listen for the right next step in order to discover something bigger and better waiting for me than I had originally planned.

Here's a crazy idea: What if we're always being guided to a better and brighter future, even when the darkness is scarier than the light? What if the pain is a necessary evil that propels and shapes us into who we're meant to become?

When we stop resisting and surrender to the possibilities that are outside what we believe to be "acceptable" or "possible," we always find ourselves at the junction of an important choice. Every Hero has at least one, whether that be the choice between your training and your friends (Luke Skywalker and Aang), or saving either the human race or your soulmate (James Cole and Neo). But how do you know which one is the correct one?

"The right ending [or choice] is the one you choose." (*12 Monkeys*)

Wait a second—so earlier in the book I told you everyone has a Destiny, and now I'm telling you that you also have a choice and free will? Am I nuts?

I'm not nuts. I just believe that two things can be true at once.

Imagine that we're all Co-Authors of our own life story and we get to write about half of it by making our own choices and impressing our desires, effectively giving our human egos a seat at the table. But we also have a separate Co-Author (AKA The Head Honcho Upstairs). Man, that guy can really be pushy sometimes. Thankfully, He's the loving kind of persistent pusher, and He has an incredibly powerful and important pen, too. In my experience, no matter how much I ignore His prompts, He always seems to be inserting the characters and plot twists required for me to choose a better version of my story than the one I've been living, just like many of my childhood heroes had to.

When Aang (*Avatar: The Last Airbender*) had to choose between his training with Guru Pathik or to save Katara, he left the Co-Author out of the equation and gave into the material fear of losing his loved one. His ultimate choice to leave ended up closing him off from the Avatar State for good, which is what everyone believed he needed to defeat the Fire Lord. And then, he got struck by lightning while trying to save everyone. Lesson learned, eh?

Thankfully, even when we ignore our Co-Author, He doesn't abandon us.

After Aang recovered, I believe his Co-Author led him to the Lion Turtle that helped him unlock his Avatar State and see another path that would allow him to stay true to himself and defeat the Fire Lord without taking his life.

Even when we don't ignore Him, but we need help, He seems to be "brainstorming" ways to help us out.

Like that time when Harry and Hermione (*Harry Potter*) were traveling to find the horcruxes. They couldn't destroy them because they needed a basilisk fang or the Sword of Gryffindor to finish the job, and the sword just happened to appear at the bottom of a lake nearby... oh, and Ron appeared at the same time, too, after a nasty breakup within the friend group.

Consider this: If we listen to His ideas before rushing to write our own, we could combine our desires and dreams to end up with a better design for our life story than what either Co-Authors had imagined independently.

In fact, the writing of this very book was a huge reminder of the need to combine wisdom.

When I started writing, I took a completely analytical approach to the themes of each chapter. I stayed in my head while I ignored the heart, refusing to connect my personal story and experiences to the lessons and insights that are conveyed. Since the beginning, my literal co-author of this book, my mom, hinted very strongly (ahem) that I should consider integrating my heart in that way; and once I finally surrendered to the possibility that my life had something to mirror—and more importantly, that it could offer readers something more powerful than I had imagined (duh)—everything clicked into place. The words and the concepts came so much easier than they had before, and

I had a chance to revisit, rewrite, and even heal my st*ries and myself.

If we co-author who we are, who we want to be, and what we want to do in alignment with the highest and best for ourselves and our fellow man, would we not be unstoppable? Who could ask for more than that?

Now, hold on there for just a minute. I didn't say this shit would be easy.

I've witnessed enough stories to know that if we dare to write our own life stories in conjunction with our Co-Author, there will be times when we need to rewrite and heal older parts of our stories that no longer serve us or are holding us back from writing a better future. This concept of story-healing is deeply rooted in the work my mom walks people through, and nobody ever *wants* to do it, even though the process is so incredibly powerful. I've experienced it several times now myself and wrote about one of my own story-healing experiences in a collaborative book on this very subject title *You Can't Make This St*ry Up: What If It's All Happening For Us?* Seriously, the resistance to story-healing/rewriting is no joke, but there always comes a point when it's absolutely necessary to rewrite an old story. And when is that? Don't worry, our Co-Author is really good at letting us know exactly when it's time... and surprise! In my experience, it's usually at the most inconvenient and perfect moments.

How lucky are we to have a Co-Author that cares so much about our final draft? Right? Right...? Anybody...? It's super easy to get angry at that guy, but He really only does it because He wants the best and brightest for our futures.

I'm convinced of it. I have way too much evidence from Story and my life to believe otherwise.

Nonetheless, before we can experience the best and the brightest, we must experience the dark. Hell, every single hero we've talked about in this book had one of these moments! Aang (*Avatar: The Last Airbender*) was struck by Azula's lightning which caused him to nearly die and become weak for several weeks, but he regained his strength and a new ability that would end the Fire Lord's terror. When Harry (*Harry Potter and the Deathly Hallows*) turned himself over to Voldemort, he expected to be killed. Instead, when Voldemort struck him, it wasn't Harry who died but the part of Voldemort that lived inside of Harry, which ultimately allowed Harry to end him once and for all. Frodo and Sam (*The Lord of the Rings*) ventured through what could only be described as Hell on (Middle) Earth—nearly dying to a spider, a volcano, and one desperate Smeagol, among many other things—yet, in the nick of time, they were able to cast the One Ring into the searing depths of Mt. Doom. Neo (*The Matrix*) traveled to the heart of Machine City and made a deal with Deus Ex Machina to defeat Agent Smith. He goes into The Matrix and is almost corrupted by the darkness of Agent Smith, but he breaks free with the help of the Oracle and defeats him. The list goes on and on and on...

But that's why I believe we're going through what we are in the world today. Darkness before the Dawn. Death and Rebirth. An opportunity to shape the world anew in an image bigger and brighter than before.

Almost as soon as we began this writing project on the topic of using Story to cultivate character and preserve freedom, life as we knew it changed. It was more than changed—sometimes, it was unrecognizable. First the pandemic, then the unrest over social injustice, followed by a painstakingly... *impassioned* election. We've had a change in leadership, we've had protests, we've been assured of a rebound; and yet many would say we've made little progress at all to quell the burden upon our communal shoulders and the anguish in our hearts. In a world "gone mad," what are we to do to lift this strain and restore humanity's hope for the future?

"Keep moving forward." (*Meet The Robinsons*)

In a world gone mad, the way we can all contribute to a better tomorrow (and stay sane!) is through the conscious sharing and consumption of Story. Because of how we've intentionally engaged story, I have had very different experiences than those of my similarly-aged peers these last few years. I've watched others make choices to affect change that I know—because I've seen them in stories—simply won't work. And worse, they may turn these intelligent and compassionate people whom I love dearly into the very thing they are seeking to change or destroy.

I'm not saying that I haven't experienced my fair share of uncertainty, of fear, of having to make seemingly impossible choices that might have led to a loss in belonging during this tumultuous time. But because of my cognizant integration with Story, I have a deeper sense of knowing that this is the "Darkness before the Dawn." That my role is to be like the heroes in training, to prepare myself and listen to myself and the wisdom around and within me. To cultivate alliances. To sort out characters who are acting like villains and who aren't. To remember I have a Destiny. And perhaps most paramount, to be the type of leader the world needs and that I want to be.

Character is cultivated with every choice, so why not make ours with the wisdom of thousands of characters and stories? Take note of the "good" choices they make, but we'd be sensible to remember the "bad" ones even more.

> *"A movie could be considered as more real than normal life. Why would you watch it otherwise? It's normal life stripped of everything that's trivial. So, is fiction more real than life? Is abstraction more real than reality? It certainly is in many cases."*
> ~ Dr. Jordan B. Peterson ~

Freedom is preserved by presenting minds and hearts the opportunity to think big, feel honestly, and take responsibility for themselves—to co-author their stories before co-authoring our collective stories.

Humanity's spirit has been trampled, scarred, and left to the proverbial dogs these last few years. Sickness, unrest, chaos, immense uncertainty. We've been disconnected and frightened, consumed by seemingly unending disaster and suffering. We've been rattled into a state of survival that feels like a macrocosm of what I had to go through those years ago.

Maybe that's what is needed for our happy ending. Maybe all of this darkness will result in a moment where we can heal our collective stories. Maybe this is an opportunity to become more than we could have ever imagined. Maybe we're being guided to the highest and best... for all of us. Maybe *Ted Lasso* was right when he said (two minutes before this book goes to publication): "Fairy tales do not start, nor do they end, at the dark forest. That's only something that shows up smack dab in the middle of the story, but it will all work out. It may not work out how you think it will or how you hope it does. But believe me, it will all work out, exactly as it's supposed to."

I truly believe that. I really do. I also believe that it's our job to not give into that darkness, because once we surrender to it instead of the better and brighter possibilities, we close ourselves off from our Co-Author and end up scrawling a terrible and destructive life story full of icky patterns that consume our spirit and our potential.

We need to stay curious and open to any invitations that may come our way. We need to write our stories collaboratively with our Co-Author, and trust Him above all tribes and earthly troubles. Engage every connection, every learning opportunity, every message inside and out as an invitation to listen and learn and write the next chapter of our life stories.

And look—I was *not* raised religious by any means. Even though I was born during a time where my parents had a falling out with Religion and to great extent God as a whole, my mom made sure I was allowed to discover who I felt and thought God to be in the way in which I was called. As a result, I can say that the power of Story has guided me to the conclusion that there is something out there *and inside us* that is guiding us to the highest and best for us and the world. When we can focus on the ultimate commonality that binds each and every one of us together (Story), when we can learn to stop making up harmful stories about each other (lies and assumptions), when we can recognize the stories behind everyone's stories, and that our stories collide for a reason, we can better navigate the suffering of life with a united front that recognizes the divinity and the potential within each and every one of us.

Our world will always be perfectly imperfect; but if we can get out of our own ways and consciously rewrite our individual and collective stories and patterns that hold us back from living Our potential, nothing can stop us from designing a future that will work for *all of us* and continually cultivate humanity into a greater version of itself.

A Special Invitation

Most of our readers asked for a compendium of our favorite stories, so we've curated a list for them and you.

You will find stories, primary themes to explore in each of them, and ratings to make it easier for you to mindfully engage Story with your child(ren).

Download it at www.SavedByStory.house/AROS-List.

Journey Through Your Religion of Story With Us!

By now, you can see how the stories you have watched, heard, and lived on and off-screen have all contributed to the lens through which you experience the world and negotiate your way through it.

Your reactions to challenges and crises, your connection to your superpowers and kryptonite, your experiences with mentors and friends, your decisions about how you engage victims and villains, your sense of purpose, and your ability to lead have not only been shaped by Story, but they are creating limited or unlimited pathways for your children's character and future.

We designed a 7-part series to help you unearth and unpack your Religion of Story, so that you can engage these themes with your children in a more intentional way through the medium of Story.

These workshops are insightful, productive, AND fun!

**Join us for the first workshop in the series
— Dive into Uncertainty With Us —
for FREE!**

**Register at to
www.SavedByStory.house/AROS-Journey.**

About
Aaron

Entrepreneurial at heart, Aaron Johnson has been both deeply involved with start-ups since he was a child and mesmerized by Story and the hero's journey. When he began paving his own non-traditional education and career paths and rediscovered some of his own potential through Improv, Debate, and Mock Trial competitions, he quickly realized that every system and solution needs to be unique because every person's vision, mission, and *path* is different.

As a Project/Administrative Manager and Tech Strategist, Aaron helps entrepreneurs discover and unleash potential in themselves and their businesses using intuitive systems and soulful technology. Seeing how crucial Community and Communication are, Aaron integrated everything he had learned about connection and leadership from mentors, personal adventures, and stories into his approach to systems, teams, and building businesses. That's when he founded his Consulting and Management company, Caterbuilder Solutions, through which he helps entrepreneurs cater to their crowd and build their dreams.

Today, he's helping build an intergenerational network of change-makers that help individuals clarify their gifts/talents and unfold their unique potential so they can be and create the change they want to see in the world. He's also collaborating with paradigm-changers to build Saved By Story Publishing — a publishing house that highlights the healing process of book writing and pushes messengers' messages further into the world. It's always more than *just* a book, which is why this is more than *just* a publishing house.

When he's not masterminding or managing, Aaron spends his time meditating on and writing about big ideas, important lessons, and the power of Story. In 2022, his healing-through-writing experience was published in *You Can't Make This St*ry Up: What If It's All Happening For Us?,* a collaboration with twenty other messengers about the transformation and divine synchronicities experienced in the creative process.

Aaron's passion lies with creating educational opportunities like he had while he was in school that value and cultivate the innate superpowers of the individual and put youth in charge of their learning journey. Participating in meaningful conversation and sparking solutions to complex problems are what keep him up at night and his flame of motivation burning.

He lives in Prescott, AZ, with his parents and his dogs Tipper and Betsy.

About
Amanda

As the founder of True To Intention and co-founder of Saved By Story Publishing, Amanda Johnson partners with seekers and storytellers devoted to writing truer individual and collective stories.

After years of helping others question, recognize, and articulate powerful messages as a Teacher and Writing Coach, Amanda uncovered her own true intention and began a lifelong quest to embody it. Alchemizing lessons, skills, and tools gathered from experiments with self-image and psycho cybernetics, the classics and the Socratic method in the honors program, the child development and psychology of learning classes in her teacher training, the social-emotional literacy workshops required to become a facilitator, and the adventures of motherhood, Amanda committed her life to changing the world with more powerful messaging. Quickly, she realized that True To Intention was more about the messenger than the message, as she witnessed individuals heal their stories as they wrote and shared them.

As a Strategist, Facilitator, Storyteller, Guide, and Ally, she midwifes paradigm-changing brands, content, and more whole change agents into the world through her st*ry-healing quests and message-manifesting retreats. From inspiration to impact, she and her team help divinely-inspired souls dissolve the lies, reorganize their sacred material, and become truer to intention with every piece of content they craft, love offering they launch, and system they structure to change the world.

In 2013, Amanda wrote *Upside-Down Mommy* and shared The Butterfly Approach philosophy responsible for her growth as a parent, messenger, and coach. In 2018, she published *Upside-Down Messenger* and made The Messenger Matrix more visible. In 2022, she published two collaborative titles: *You Can't Make This St*ry Up* is a collaboration with twenty of her clients curated to help creatives and coaches recognize and lean into the magic and mess of becoming a powerful change agent, and *A Religion of Story* is a collaboration with her son crafted to share the experience and results of mindfully engaging Story to cultivate character and agency in children and culture.

As a momma, a wife, a messenger, an entrepreneur, and a friend, Amanda is determined to empower a generation that challenges the narratives handed to them with curiosity and love, heals the st*ries that hold us back, and co-authors a messy magically-ever-after.

Made in the USA
Monee, IL
01 July 2022

98925782R00152